A PATH THROUGH SUFFERING

A PATH THROUGH SUFFERING

Elisabeth Elliot

Regal

From Gospel Light
Ventura, California, U.S.A.

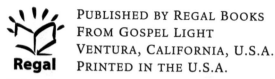

PUBLISHED BY REGAL BOOKS
FROM GOSPEL LIGHT
VENTURA, CALIFORNIA, U.S.A.
PRINTED IN THE U.S.A.

Regal Books is a ministry of Gospel Light, a Christian publisher dedicated to serving the local church. We believe God's vision for Gospel Light is to provide church leaders with biblical, user-friendly materials that will help them evangelize, disciple and minister to children, youth and families.

It is our prayer that this Regal book will help you discover biblical truth for your own life and help you meet the needs of others. May God richly bless you.

For a free catalog of resources from Regal Books/Gospel Light, please call your Christian supplier or contact us at 1-800-4-GOSPEL *or* www.regalbooks.com.

Originally published by Servant Publications in 1990.

All Scripture quotations are taken from *The New English Bible.* © The Delegates of Oxford University Press and The Syndics of the Cambridge University Press 1961, 1970, 1989. Reprinted by permission.

Cover design by Michael Andaloro
Illustrations by James N. Howard

Library of Congress Cataloging-in-Publication Data

Elliot, Elisabeth.
  A path through suffering / Elisabeth Elliot.
    p. cm.
  Originally published: Ann Arbor, Mich. : Vine Books, 1990.
  ISBN 0-8307-3469-4
  1. Suffering—Religious aspects—Christianity—Meditations. I. Title.
  BV4909.E45 2004
  242'.4—dc22   2003028065

1 2 3 4 5 6 7 8 9 10 11 12 13 14 15 / 09 08 07 06 05 04

Rights for publishing this book in other languages are contracted by Gospel Light Worldwide, the international nonprofit ministry of Gospel Light. Gospel Light Worldwide also provides publishing and technical assistance to international publishers dedicated to producing Sunday School and Vacation Bible School curricula and books in the languages of the world. For additional information, visit www.gospellightworldwide.org; write to Gospel Light Worldwide, P.O. Box 3875, Ventura, CA 93006; or send an e-mail to info@gospellightworldwide.org.

AUTHOR'S NOTE

Pronouns referring to the divinity are capitalized except in quotations from Scripture. In my opinion this makes for clarity.

Other books by Elisabeth Elliot

A Lamp for My Feet
Love Has a Price Tag
The Liberty of Obedience
The Savage My Kinsman
Shadow of the Almighty
These Strange Ashes
Let Me Be a Woman
The Mark of a Man
Passion and Purity
Discipline: The Glad Surrender
Loneliness
On Asking God Why
A Chance to Die: The Life and
   Legacy of Amy Carmichael

To Bunny
(Elizabeth Paeth Lasker)

who, as physician, has given so much more than medicine;
as mother of five knows the suffering and the courage of love;
and as my friend has understood.

Contents

ACKNOWLEDGMENTS

My sincere thanks are due to Ann Spangler and Mary Case of Servant Publications for their help, and to all who generously allowed me to use their stories.

Preface

AMONG THE VISITORS TO ISAK DINESEN'S FARM in Africa in the 1930s was a wandering Swede named Emmanuelson, who claimed to be a tragic actor. He spent one night and set off on foot the next morning for Tanganyika in spite of his hostess's warning that that was "not a possible thing to do for anyone." There was no water in the Masai Reserve and the lions were "bad" there at that time. She heard from him later, however, that he had made it to Tanganyika and on his way had been very kindly treated by the Masai.

"It was fit and becoming, I thought, that Emmanuelson should have sought refuge with the Masai," Dinesen wrote in *Out of Africa*, "and that they should have received him. The true aristocracy and the true proletariat of the world are both in understanding with tragedy. To them it is a fundamental principle of God and the key—the minor key—to existence. They differ in this way from the bourgeoisie of all classes, who deny tragedy, who will not tolerate it, and to whom the world of tragedy means itself unpleasantness."

Perhaps this is just the key we have lost. Suffering, even in its mildest forms—inconvenience, delay, disappointment, discomfort, or anything that is not in harmony with our whims and preferences—we will not tolerate. We even reject and deny it. Stress is the result, and stress, I believe, afflicts primarily those whom Dinesen would call the bourgeoisie.

🌿

Have we missed a fundamental principle of God? Is not suffering, loss, even death itself the minor key to existence? Do we not lose our very lives by trying so hard to save them?

Being neither a theologian nor a scholar has not prevented me from pondering the principle. The measure of pain in my own life (negligible compared with the sufferings I hear about) has been sufficient to pose the question of the meaning of suffering.

> Is there not wrong too bitter for atoning?
> What are these desperate and hideous years?
> Hast Thou not heard Thy whole creation groaning,
> Sighs of a bondsman and a woman's tears?
>
> (F.W.H. Meyers: *St. Paul*)

The words which have illuminated for me the deepest understanding of suffering are Jesus' own, "In truth, in very truth I tell you, a grain of wheat remains a solitary grain unless it falls into the ground and dies; but if it dies, it bears a rich harvest." This, He told His disciples, was the key. *There is a necessary link between suffering and glory.*

But what difference does that make in the life of an ordinary man or woman? (This is the question I am always asking myself as I read the Bible or books about the Bible, as I hear a spiritual talk or as I try to talk to others about spiritual things: what *difference* ought this to make in the way I live?)

Two little books, now out of print, wonderfully expand on the imagery Jesus used, and have greatly helped me to understand the principle. They are Lilias Trotter's *Parables of the Cross* and *Parables of the Christ-Life*.

Lilias Trotter was born in London in 1853, seventh child of a businessman. She was tall and slender with large brown eyes, an active and orderly mind, and "a quality of selflessness which gave her a peculiar charm." When she was twenty-three she met John Ruskin in Venice, who recognized her gift for painting and offered to give her lessons. "She seemed to learn everything the instant she was shown it," he wrote, "and ever so much more than she was taught." But her heart was elsewhere. She had put herself, her gifts, her life at God's disposal, so it was a great disappointment to Ruskin and a surprise to others when she decided to give herself to missionary work. She was criticized and even ostracized, but her enthusiasm was fed, not quenched, by scorn.

For some reason, North Africa awakened strange vibrations in her soul. She heard what she believed was God's specific call, and in 1888 landed in Algiers, where she spent the rest of her life. She was the founder of the Algiers Mission Band which later merged with the North Africa Mission. She died in 1928.

She found in the plant life of the deserts the fundamental principle of existence—that death is the gateway to life—exhibited in a thousand ways, and painted them with her brush and watercolors. Who is to say she was a fool for turning her back on home, the possibilities of marriage and perhaps an artist's career (these, after all, were certainly God's good gifts)? The last of her water colors in *Parables of the Cross* is that of the wood sorrel, springing from an apparently useless little pile of twigs and dead leaves. She writes, "God may use . . . the things that He has wrought in us, for the blessings of souls unknown to us: as these twigs and leaves of bygone years, whose individuality is forgotten, pass on vitality still to the newborn wood sorrel. God only knows the endless possibilities that lie folded in each one of us!"

"Shall we not go all lengths with Him in His plans for us—not, as these 'green things upon the earth' in their unconsciousness, but with the glory of free choice? Shall we not translate the story of their little lives into our own?"

I am one of those souls unknown to Lilias Trotter, blessed by her surrender and sacrifice—no "fanciful mysticism," but a spiritual reality that can be tested at every turn.

Readers may find that one chapter is enough (or more than enough) for one day's reading. The excerpts from the parables which head each chapter bear rich food for meditation. May the Lord enable us to translate them into practical reality as we contemplate the fact of suffering.

Magnolia, Massachusetts
June 1990

ONE

The Sign of the Cross

an we not trace the sign of the Cross in the first hint of the new spring's dawning? In many cases, as in the chestnut, before a single leaf has faded, next year's buds may be seen at the summit of branch and twig, formed into its very stem blood-red.

Back in the plant's first stages, the crimson touch is to be found in seed-leaves and fresh shoots, and even in hidden sprouts. Look at the acorn, for instance, as it breaks its shell, and see how the baby tree bears its birthmark.

A SIX-YEAR-OLD BOY WROTE TO ME, "My grandmother has a brain tumor. The doctor says she only has six months to live. Can you help me about this?" He enclosed a picture of himself. I held it in my hand and studied the little face—so sweet, so wistful. Could I help him about this?

It was not the first time I had faced such a question. What was I, a jungle missionary, to say to my own child of two when she learned the song "Jesus Loves Me" and wanted to know whether Jesus had loved her daddy too? I gave her the truth: yes. Next question: Then why did He let the Auca Indians kill him? A little girl can be shown that her father's death is a gateway to life for him, but how was I to explain the truth of the *delivering* power of death? I could not. But I still had to give an answer, a truthful answer: I did not know *all* God's reasons. The ones I was quite sure I did know Valerie could not have understood then. But that He *had* reasons, I was sure. That they were loving reasons I was also sure. The assurance that it was *not for nothing* comforted me and I gave my peace to my child.

I had had occasion to ask the same questions when I was small. Our mother and father sang us to sleep with songs like

Safe in the arms of Jesus,
Safe on His gentle breast,
There by His love o'ershaded,
Sweetly my soul shall rest.   (Fanny J. Crosby)

and:

Jesus, tender Shepherd, hear me,
Bless Thy little lamb tonight,
Through the darkness be Thou near me,
Keep me safe 'til morning light.   (Mary Duncan)

But then I was greatly frightened by the kidnapping of the famous Charles Lindbergh's baby. Did Jesus not love him?

A missionary who had been a guest in our home when I was about four had her head chopped off by Chinese Communists when I was eight. I have never forgotten the newspaper picture of her orphaned baby, peeping out of a rice basket carried by the Chinese Christian who had found her. Jesus lets missionaries be killed. Jesus lets babies lose their parents.

Essie McCutcheon was my very lively childhood friend. She had me panting to keep up as she raced through other people's backyards and alleyways. She stood my hair on end with her imaginative stories—a giant with a match the size of a telephone pole who burned down the house next door, a corpse she found under the back porch. We were the same age, but she was way ahead of me—she would get her baby brother up in the morning, change him, lug him to the kitchen, fix his breakfast and everybody else's. All that energy and imagination and know-how! When we were both nine years old Essie was very sick in the hospital. Her sisters and parents, my brothers and my parents and I all prayed that the Lord would heal her. He could do that, we knew. But Essie died. Jesus lets children lose their best friends.

Repeatedly throughout our lives we encounter the roadblock of suffering. What do we do with it? Our answer will determine what we can say to another who needs comfort. How was I to reply to the little boy about his grandmother? Should I just give him a few Scripture verses and leave it at that? These, perhaps?

> For you, the Lord is a safe retreat;
> you have made the Most High your refuge.
> No disaster shall befall you,
> no calamity shall come upon your home. (Ps 91:9-10)

I know of no answer to give to anyone except the answer given to all the world in the cross. It was there that the great Grain of Wheat died—not that death should be the end of the story, but that it should be the beginning of the story, as it is in all the cycles of nature. The grain dies. The harvest results. The sun must die in the west if it is to rise in the east. The crimson touch must be found even in the fresh shoots of the baby oak—they are destined for death.

So in the early springtime of his life my young correspondent must begin to trace the sign of the cross. Of course I could not unfold to him all that I have learned through the parables of plant life (and how much more there is that I have yet to learn!). It is a long road to understanding the love of God in and through our own suffering, but I could take that little boy to the proof of Jesus' love, the cross, which towers over all the "wrecks of time," stands stark and irrefutable against all the tragedy of the world. I could tell him that Jesus really does love his grandmother and loves him. He could be absolutely sure about that because Jesus had died for them.

I can still hear Essie singing her favorite chorus:

Everybody ought to love Jesus, Jesus, Jesus—
He died on the cross to save us from sin.
Everybody ought to love Jesus.

The song had a logical idea and a bouncy tune. But suffering takes us far below tunes and logic. Who of us has not known the confusion, the ambivalence, the restlessness of pain? The soul is a kingdom divided against itself. Job cried out in anguish from his ash heap. Israel complained against the Lord and blamed Moses. Moses brought their complaints and quite a few of his own to the Lord—why, why, why? Our Lord Jesus Himself wrestled with His will ("If it is possible . . . If it is not possible . . . *not* my will but Thine be done").

I think I must have asked Jesus to be my Savior at a very

early age. It would have been natural to do so, given the godly training I had. I have no recollection of not being a Christian. But when I was ten years old I heard a sermon on the words, "You must be born again." Had I been? Not certain, I stood when the invitation was given to declare publicly that I wanted to be. Two or three years later I learned that Jesus must be not only Savior but Lord. I wanted that too, and prayed a prayer of commitment written by Betty Scott Stam, the missionary who had been beheaded, surrendering all my plans, purposes, desires, and hopes, myself, my life, my all, to God to be His forever. I asked Him to work out His whole will in my life, at any cost.

In the decisions made at ten or twelve I did not clearly see the life-out-of-death principle. Of course I didn't. As someone has written, death is the only way out of any world in which we are. The newborn baby dies a death to the safe, warm life of the womb. The reborn Christian forsakes the old life, "dies" to it, and receives the life of Christ in its place. The surrender of one's will—what could be more certainly a death? But it is the condition of receiving God's will, God's life, God's joy.

There is no question in my mind that God pays attention to such prayers, even if they are prayed by a child. Never mind that we do not know what we are asking. He knows. He knows our frame, too, and remembers that we are dust, so He leads us tenderly and carefully along the pathway we have chosen, which is the way of the cross.

When I was fourteen or so I began to think seriously about the words to one of my favorite hymns, "Beneath the cross of Jesus I fain would take my stand." What, exactly, did that mean? Was I willing to accept *only* the sunshine of Christ's face (when I could think of all kinds of "sunshine" I hoped for), to "know no gain or loss" (I had several ambitions)? I wanted to be willing. It was going to take some learning.

In college I learned to love Lucy A. Bennett's hymn, "O teach me what it meaneth, that cross uplifted high" (Hymns, Inter-Varsity Press, Chicago 1969). Would God not begin to do just that if I asked Him to?

He began. The first place the cross touched me in a way that cut deeply was in my heart's desire for marriage. I fell in love with a man in college who had believed that God wanted him to remain single, perhaps for life, but at least until he had had experience in jungle missionary work. Here was my chance to learn what death was about—death to myself—and to take up the cross, that is, willingly to accept the will of God which went so strongly against the grain of my own. It was not easy. Jesus never suggested that it should be. Amy Carmichael's poem helped me to be specific:

Lord Crucified, O mark Thy holy Cross
On motive, preference, all fond desires,
On that which self in any form inspires,
Set Thou that sign of loss.

And when the touch of death is here and there
Laid on a thing most precious in our eyes,
Let us not wonder, let us recognize
The answer to this prayer.   (Toward Jerusalem
                               Christian Literature Crusade
                               Ft. Washington, PA 1988, p. 96)

The cross means suffering. Suffering's meaning is to be learned through the cross.

🌱

TWO

A Clean Severance

otanists say that across the leaf-stalk there forms in autumn a layer of thin-walled cells, termed "the layer of separation." These press and tear the older cells apart, and become disintegrated in their turn, till without an effort the leaf detaches with a severance clean and sharp as though made by a knife. The plant sentences the leaf to death, and the winds of God carry out the sentence

IN OLD TESTAMENT TIMES suffering was seen as evil. In the New Testament, suffering and evil are no longer identical. Think of the shock the crowds must have felt when Jesus said that those who mourn, those who are poor and persecuted and have nothing are *happy*! How could He say such things? Only in light of another kingdom, another world, another way of seeing this world. He came to bring life—another kind of life altogether. And it is in terms of that life that we must learn to look at our sufferings. I have found it possible, when I see suffering from that perspective, wholeheartedly to *accept* it. But it takes a steady fixing of my gaze on the cross.

If the cross is the place where the worst thing that could happen happened, it is also the place where the best thing that could happen happened. Ultimate hatred and ultimate love met on those two crosspieces of wood. Suffering and love were brought into harmony.

It was while we were still powerless to help ourselves that Jesus died for us. It is a rare thing, as Paul points out, for anybody to die even for a good man, "but Christ died for us while we were yet sinners, and that is God's own proof of his love towards us. And so, since we have now been justified by Christ's sacrificial death, we shall all the more certainly be saved through him from final retribution" (Rom 5:8-9).

To be "saved" requires a severance from the former life as clean and sharp as though made by a knife. There must be a wall of separation between the old life and the new, a radical break. That means death—death to the old life, in order for the new to begin. "We know that the man we once were has been crucified with Christ, for the destruction of the sinful self, so that we may no longer be the slaves of sin, since a dead man is no longer answerable for his sin" (Rom 6:6-7).

This wall of separation, this barrier, is the cross.

From earliest memory I understood that everybody ought to love Jesus. Then I began to hear that everybody ought to "receive the Lord Jesus Christ as his own personal Savior." To the best of my understanding that is what I wanted to do, so I did it—I asked Him to come into my heart, as I was instructed to do. It was a once-for-all decision, and I believe He accepted the invitation and came in. So far so good. I was told that I was now "saved," saved by grace. That was a gift, a free gift, from God. Amazing. Simply amazing that the Lord of the Universe, the One who is "the ruler over all authorities and the supreme head over all powers" (Col 2:10, JBP), "the blessed controller of all things, the king over all kings and the master of all masters, the only source of immortality, the One who lives in unapproachable light, the One whom no mortal eye has ever seen or ever can see" (1 Tm 6:15-16, JBP)—amazing that the same One bends His ear to the prayer of a child or of a sinner of any age and, if asked, comes in and makes His home with us. For His name is Immanuel, *God* with *us*.

How shall He be at home with us unless our lives are in harmony with His holy life? Unless He lives His very life in us and we live our lives "in company with Him"? Salvation means *rescue* from the pit of destruction, from the miry clay of ourselves.

So my decision to receive Him, although made only once, I must affirm in thousands of ways, through thousands of choices, for the rest of my life—my will or His, my life (the old one) or His (the new one). It is no to myself and yes to Him. This continual affirmation is usually made in small things, inconveniences, unselfish giving up of preferences, yielding gracefully to the wishes of others without playing the martyr, learning to close doors quietly and turn the volume down on the music we'd love to play loudly—sufferings they may be, but only small-sized ones. We may think of them as little "deaths."

Many who come to Christ have a long, sinful, and destructive past. The "layer of separation," the cross, stands now between us and our past. We have to make up our minds to part company with it, not by struggle but by an honest act of renouncing it in the name of Christ. Sin no longer holds authority, "exacting obedience to the body's desires. You must no longer put its several parts at sin's disposal, as implements for doing wrong. No: put yourselves at the disposal of God, as dead men raised to life; yield your bodies to him as implements for doing right; for sin shall no longer be your master, because you are no longer under law, but under the grace of God" (Rom 6:12-14).

When Satan the accuser scorns that act of renunciation later and taunts—"Hypocrite! You didn't mean it! You never *really* put yourself at His disposal or parted company with us at all!"—run to the foot of the cross, our safe shelter and abiding place.

The further we travel on this pathway to glory the more glorious it becomes, because we are given to understand that every glad surrender of self, which to the young Christian may seem such a morbid and odious thing, is merely a little death, like the tree's "loss" of the dead leaf, in order that a fresh new one may, in God's time, take its place.

The New Leaf

rom the first hour that the layer of separation begins to form in the leafstalk, the leaf's fate is sealed; there is never a moment's reversal of the decision. Each day that follows is a steady carrying out of the plant's purpose: "This old leaf shall die, and the new leaf shall live."

MY FRIEND TERRI KNOTT BECAME A CHRISTIAN when she was a teenager. For a while the change was not a dramatic one, but she began studying the Bible and trying to live like a Christian. There had been certain tensions between her and her mother—"typical sixteen-year-old kinds of things," she says, "missing a curfew here and there, getting a speeding ticket a block from my house, not calling home to tell my parents I'd be late."

One day Terri discovered that, according to God's Word, she was supposed to "honor" her parents. What, exactly, did that mean? She thought about it. She prayed about it. She did not relish the answer she got, for it meant a kind of death—

she was going to have to submit to them. Becoming a Christian means submission to God, which almost always, in one way or another, means submission to somebody He has put over us. Alas. Who of us likes to submit? Terri was not eager to do this, but she was eager to know God and to do what He said. Because she loved Him, she accepted this very personal, very practical death to the "old leaf," and she asked for His help.

The day came when she asked permission to go to a party given by someone her mother did not know. "The case was highly scrutinized," Terry said, and her mother's answer was no. Terri's response startled both of them. Instead of the usual argument, a quiet "Okay." A "new leaf" had actually begun to appear.

She went to her room, sat down on a chair, and said, "I can't believe what just happened! Mother said no and I said okay! I didn't even *argue* with her! I didn't even raise my *voice!* I . . . I guess that's 'honoring' your mother, isn't it, Lord? Well, thank You. Thank You for helping me."

Not a moment's reversal of the decision. A steady carrying out of her purpose to live as a Christian. It didn't happen in an instant. It wasn't the last crisis she'd face. It was one thing God had shown her had to change and with His help she changed it. The self-life—doing her own thing—had to go. She could not do it by herself, but she could *will* to do it, and she could pray. She asked for God's help and she got it. Grace enables us to do what we can't do.

Many of our sufferings are of our own making. If Terri had decided she was old enough to make her own decisions and God's Word did not apply in her case, tensions would have increased and suffering would have been prolonged. Obedi-

❧

ence freed her. And so it is with all of us. A recalcitrant child of God brings upon himself troubles he need never have had, as Scripture says, "The way of transgressors is hard" (Prv 13:15, AV).

> Oh, what peace we often forfeit,
> Oh, what needless pain we bear,
> All because we do not carry
> Everything to God in prayer. (Joseph Scrivin)

If Terri had tried to change all by herself she would have experienced frustration. But it would have been *needless* pain. Instead, she carried the situation to God.

Pride is at the root of all sins, and it is pride that often keeps us from carrying things to God in prayer. We imagine we can handle things quite well on our own, or we fear that God is likely to tell us to do something we don't want to do. (He *is* likely to do that, as He did in Terri's case, because He loves us.) The whole Christian life is a process of bringing the self-life down to death in order that the life of Jesus may be manifest in us. "As he grows greater, I must grow less," said John the Baptist (Jn 3:30).

"Let us remember that it is not God who makes many of the crosses that we find in our way, such as we commonly call 'crosses.' Our Heavenly Father makes 'straight paths for our feet,'... But when the path that God points out goes north and south, and our stubborn wills lead us east and west, the consequence is '*a cross*'—a cross of our own making, not that which our Master bids us 'take up and carry after Him,' and of which it has been well said, 'He always carries the heaviest end Himself'" (Annie Webb-Peploe, quoted in Mary Tileston: *Joy and Strength,* World Wide Publications, Minneapolis 1986, p. 354).

To a heart willing to be shown, God will reveal the self-inflicted causes of trouble. There are many examples given in Scripture, such as receiving the Lord's Supper in an unworthy manner (1 Cor 11:27-30), persistence in sin (1 Pt 4:17), and—this is the reason for prolonged and terrible miseries—a refusal to forgive (Mt 18:34-35).

One day recently something lit a fuse of anger in someone who then burned me with hot words. I felt sure I did not deserve this response, but when I ran to God about it, He reminded me of part of a prayer I had been using: "Teach me to treat all that comes to me with peace of soul and with firm conviction that Your will governs all."

His will that I should be burned? Not exactly, but His will *governs* all. In a wrong-filled world we suffer (and cause) many a wrong. God is there to heal and comfort and forgive. He who brought blessing to many out of the sin of the jealous brothers against Joseph means this hurt for my ultimate blessing and, I think, for an increase of love between me and the one who hurt me. Love is very patient, very kind. Love never seeks its own good. Love looks to God for grace to help.

"It was not you who sent me here but God," Joseph said to the brothers who had meant to get rid of him altogether. "You meant to do me harm, but God meant to bring good out of it" (Gn 45:8; 50:20). Here is consolation for us when someone sins against us: God sent it, and God meant it—for good.

When we pray, "Give us this day our daily bread," an angry retort from someone may be part of the answer, for it may furnish just the occasion we need in which to learn not only longsuffering and forgiveness, but meekness, gentleness, fruits not *born* in us but *borne* only by the Spirit in us. Amy Carmichael wrote, "A cup brimful of sweetness cannot spill even one drop of bitter water, no matter how suddenly jarred."

All this is part of the process of separating us from the old life and forming in us the new. Painful it must be, of course, but look to the purpose! Look to the glory God has in mind, accept it, and say with the psalmist, "I, thy servant, will study thy statutes. Thy instruction is my continual delight; I turn to it for counsel. . . . I will run the course set out in thy command-ments, *for they gladden my heart*" (Ps 119:23-24, 32, italics mine).

FOUR

Spiritual Pruning

t is when the death of winter has done its work that the sun can draw out in each plant its own individuality, and make its existence full and fragrant. Spiritual growth means something more than the sweeping away of the old leaves of sin—it means the life of the Lord Jesus developed in us.

IN GOD'S MANAGEMENT OF THE AFFAIRS OF MEN suffering is never senseless. We can find plenty of good sense in the metaphor of pruning found in the Gospel of John.

When Jesus was about to say farewell to His disciples, He was straightforward with them about what they should expect when He was gone. They would face much suffering. They would be hated as He had been. They would be persecuted. People would follow their teaching as little as they had followed His. They would be banned from the synagogues and even killed by those who believed that killing them was a special service to God.

Jesus explained His reason for giving them all this bad news:

it was so that their faith *in Him* would not be shaken. Faith in anything less would certainly collapse, but a strong and settled trust in who He is would not be altered by anything that might happen. It was for them to continue His work, represent Him on earth, be the very bearers of the divine life when the Word Himself was taken away.

And how were they to do this? They would have to *dwell* in Him—abide, remain, make their home in, stay—sharing His life, drawing His strength. The secret was explained to them not theoretically but analogically. Their relationship to Him was that of branches to a vine. The life of the vine is the life of the branch. It has no other life. As long as the branch remains in the vine it is nourished. Cut off, it dies.

"Apart from Me you can do nothing." In the spiritual realm there is no other life but Christ's. In Him we live. Without Him we die.

Vines must be pruned. This looks like a cruel business. Perfectly good branches have to be lopped off in order for better branches to develop. It is a necessary business, for only the well-pruned vine bears the best fruit. The life of the vine is strengthened in one part by another part's being cut away. The rank growth has to go and then the sun reaches places it could not reach before. Pruning increases yield.

So also in the spiritual life. We may pray a prayer such as Lancelot Andrewes prayed in the seventeenth century: "O direct my life towards Thy commandments, hallow my soul, purify my body, correct my thoughts, cleanse my desires, soul and body, mind and spirit, heart and reins. Renew me thoroughly, O Lord, for if Thou wilt Thou canst" (*Lancelot Andrewes and His Private Devotions*).

I think again of Terri. I don't suppose she was making use of

Andrewes's prayer, but she certainly wanted exactly what he wanted. And God heard her and began the process of directing this teenage girl towards His commandments. Some old twigs and branches had to go. When we ask for the hallowing of our souls, the correction of our thoughts, and all the rest, we are asking that the life of the Lord Jesus flow freely in us and develop His graces in us. Ought we then to be surprised that spiritual pruning will be required? When it happens, we need to submit humbly, trusting the skill of the Gardener who prunes us with tenderness.

Tenderness?

A pastor's wife asked, "When one witnesses a work he has poured his life into 'go up in flames' (especially if he is not culpable), is it the work of Satan or the hand of God?"

I looked where I always look for clues—to the Bible, and I thought of Moses' repeated efforts to persuade Pharaoh to let the people go, of Jeremiah's pleas for repentance, of the good king Josiah's reforms, rewarded in the end by his being slain by a pagan king. I thought of the beloved Son, despised and rejected. "The world, though it owed its being to him, did not recognize him. He entered his own realm, and his own would not receive him" (Jn 1:10-11).

Satan was certainly at work in every case, but he was not the only one at work. When a man or woman belongs to God (when the branch dwells in the Vine) it is the hand of God at work when the pruning comes, regardless of the second causes. A life's work—what to us is a perfectly good branch, perhaps the only "important" branch—may be cut off. The loss seems a terrible thing, a useless waste. But whose work was it? This is a question I have had to ask a number of times about work which I had thought of as my vocation, my *life's* work, apparently thrown on the brushpile. Was it not work given *by* God in the first place, then given back *to* Him day by day? Jesus said God is the Gardener, the One who takes care of the vines. The hand of the Gardener holds the knife. It is *His* glory that is at stake when the best grapes are produced, so we need not think He has something personal against us, or has left us wholly to the mercy of His enemy Satan. He is always and forever *for* us.

So we let go our hold of things we held very dear. Things that once were counted as gain we now count as loss, and out of what seems emptiness come beauty and richness. "Those who receive ... God's grace, and his gift of righteousness, live and reign through the one man, Jesus Christ" (Rom 5:17). The branches "live and reign" through the Vine.

But oh, the pain of that pruning process! No matter how thoroughly we understand its necessity, it comes hard to human flesh and blood. Yet the hardness is softened (believe me, it *is*) as we concentrate on the truth the Lord has given us:

"If you dwell in me and my words dwell in you, ask what you will, and you shall have it. This is my Father's glory, that you may bear fruit in plenty and so be my disciples. ... If you heed my commands, you will dwell in my love, as I have heeded my Father's commands and dwell in his love." Pruning leads to *joy*. "I have spoken thus to you, so that my *joy* may be in you, and your joy *complete*" (Jn 15:7-11).

There are paradoxes, of course, which we cannot plumb. Analogies break down. But we can always look at the experiences of our lives in the light of the life of our Lord Jesus, who "learned obedience," not by the things He enjoyed, but by the things He suffered. Was there suffering in His life? A great deal. Losses? All kinds. Was it *His* glory that was at stake? No, His single aim was to glorify His Father, and He did just that, every

❧

moment of His life. The work He did was the work He saw His Father do. The words He spoke were the words His Father had given Him. The purpose of His coming was to fulfill the will of the Father. His death was because He loved the Father. There was no thought of Himself.

He accepted suffering. He willingly laid down His life. He poured out His very soul unto death. Shall not we, His servants, tread the same pathway?

To "abide in the Vine" is to live our lives in Christ, living each event—a mother's wise refusal of a teenager's desire, or a life's work going up in flames—as Christ lived, in the peace of the Father's will. Did the earthly life of our Lord appear to be a thundering success? Would the statistics of souls won, crowds made into faithful disciples, sermons heeded, commands obeyed, be impressive? Hardly. In the end they all forsook Him and fled. Yet Peter, one who miserably denied Him at the last, repented with tears and later saw clearly what had taken place: "This man, who was put into your power by the predetermined plan and foreknowledge of God, you nailed up and murdered. . . . But God would not allow the bitter pains of death to hold him. He raised him to life again—and indeed there was nothing by which death could hold such a man" (Acts 2:23-24, JBP).

There is nothing by which death can hold any of His faithful servants, either. Settle it, once for all—we can never lose what we have offered to Christ. We live and die in Him, and there is always the resurrection.

FIVE

Life Out of Death

*N*ote this bit of gorse bush. *The whole year round the thorn has been hardening and sharpening. Spring comes; the thorn does not drop off and it does not soften. There it is, as uncompromising as ever, but half-way up appear two brown furry balls, mere specks at first, that break at last—straight out of last year's thorn—into a blaze of fragrant golden glory!*

The painting that accompanies Lilias Trotter's words shows a branch bristling with thorns large and small sticking out in all directions, but the yellow flowers have found a way to unfold themselves in this impossibly hostile environment.

I walked for hours one day along the cliffs of Bournemouth, England, where the gorse grows in profusion. It was wintertime, cold and raw, with gray skies and a gray sea. The gorse bushes appeared lifeless, but invisible things were happening—thorns busily being hardened and sharpened, the specks already in their appointed places out of which were to spring the furry balls. The death of wintertime is the necessary prelude to the resurrection of springtime.

Thousands have found solace in the deep spiritual lessons to be found so unmistakably in nature's ceaseless cycle of life and death. I say "unmistakably," but I would not have seen them myself without the help of many with clearer vision than I. As a teenager I read Amy Carmichael's biography of Thomas Walker of Tinnevelly. The words which were left indelibly in my mind were those of Jesus just before He went to the cross, quoted by Walker as the only plan which ensures success: "Except a corn of wheat fall into the ground and die, it abideth alone: but if it die it bringeth forth much fruit" (Jn 12:24, AV). Each time I hear or read those words they come alive for me because Thomas Walker and Amy Carmichael both staked their lives on them, willing to be a corn of wheat, embrace what is contrary to human nature, and be "buried" in South India in order that others might find the true life. When, by my own faults and indifference, or the distractions of the world, I have drifted from this changeless principle (and imagined that I might *avoid* the deaths and still somehow be fruitful) the words have rung again in the ears of my soul, *if it die, if it die, if it die.*

Lilias Trotter too needed help from others, and drew on their insights. One of those was F.W.H. Meyers, whose poem "St. Paul" she quotes, lettering into the painting of the gorse bush his words, "setteth in pain the jewel of His joy." She took them from this stanza:

> God, who whatever frenzy of our fretting
> Vexes sad life to spoil and to destroy,
> Lendeth an hour for peace and for forgetting,
> Setteth in pain the jewel of His joy.

We know very little of others' sufferings. How I would love to be allowed to look deeper into the life of Meyers, for example, and know in what sort of pain the Lord had set for him the jewel of His joy. I do not know. But I am sure the spiritual insight did not come without high cost. He must have died many deaths before he was qualified to write that long and powerful poem about the apostle's life.

So here it is—in the gorse blossoming from thorns, in the harvest of wheat from the solitary grain—the *gospel*, the Good News of life out of death, a gospel for every individual, every need, every hopeless and helpless situation.

"It'll never work for mine," someone is tempted to say. Are you sure that your problems baffle the One who since the world began has been bringing flowers from thorns? Your thorns are a different story, are they? You have been brought to a place of self-despair, nothingness. It is hard even to think of any good reason for going on. You live in most unfavorable conditions, with intractable people, you are up against impossible odds. Is this something new? The people of Israel were up against impossible odds when they found themselves between the chariots of Egypt and the Red Sea. Their God is our God. The God of Israel and the God of the gorse thorns looks down on us with love and says, "Nothing has happened to you which is not common to all. I can manage it. Trust Me."

He wants to transform every form of human suffering into something glorious. He can redeem it. He can bring life out of death. Every event of our lives provides opportunity to learn the deepest lesson anyone can learn on earth, "My present life is not that of the old 'I,' but the living Christ within me" (Gal 2:20, JBP). When our souls lie barren in a winter which seems hopeless and endless, God has not abandoned us. His work goes on. He asks our acceptance of the painful process and our trust that He will indeed give resurrection life.

How often I am troubled about something that looms ahead, wondering how I am to cope when the time comes. Why do I not bring it at once to the Lord, who stands ready with the *next grace* for the *next thing?* Why is it so easy to forget His simple word, "If you need wisdom, I'll give it to you. If you need strength, it will be there in exact proportion to the difficulties of the day. If you need guidance, I'm your Shepherd. If you need comfort, My name is Comforter."

Corrie Ten Boom was a woman of strong faith and a radiant face. Why? Not because she had not suffered, but because she had, and had responded to that suffering (in a concentration camp during World War II) with trust. Learning the depth of human helplessness and weakness, she turned to her "strong tower" and He was faithful to His promises.

One of the most soul-fortifying pictures I have of her in my mind is of her getting up in the morning, standing up in her solitary cell, and singing in a loud voice so that other prisoners could hear, "Stand up, stand up for Jesus!"

"Oh, I could never have survived," we say. Well, we were not asked to. But we could have *if* the Lord had allowed us to be put in her position, and *if* we had responded as Corrie did, looking to Him for the next grace. I mean, of course, that we could have survived spiritually. The body they may kill, but so what? Jesus said, "Do not fear those who kill the body and after that have nothing more they can do. I will warn you whom to fear: fear him who, after he has killed, has authority to cast into hell" (Lk 12:5). In other words, fear God and become fearless. Nothing in heaven or earth or hell can scare you.

The experience of weakness puts us in the position of seeking another's strength. Paul the apostle had his own particular thorn, translated in one version as "a sharp physical

❧

pain." It came as Satan's messenger to bruise him, and he prayed three times for its removal. Suppose the gorse bush were to ask that the thorns be removed so that it might bear lovely yellow flowers? It doesn't work that way. God said no to Paul's plea because he was to bring forth, for the sake of the rest of us, the beautiful flower of acceptance, a gift of grace, *enough* for his need. But that flower was to bloom, not in spite of, but because of the thorn. Paul probably did not see the tiny "specks" which were to break out into a blaze of fragrant, golden glory. Could he know of the millions who would be cheered and comforted by his example of quiet acceptance of a painful thing which he knew God could have removed? No, he couldn't. It was not his business to know. He was simply to accept the answer given—grace, in the measure needed.

When in pain it is hard to think of anything but pain. Amy Carmichael wrote of being so weak she could not think or pray, but she took comfort from the psalm, "Let the lifting up of my hands be as the evening sacrifice" (Ps 141:2, AV). She was able simply to lift them to the Lord—a gesture of acceptance, of adoration, of faith. We have our Father's promise, linking the pain to an unimaginable glory: "If we suffer, we shall also reign with him" (2 Tm 2:12).

SIX

Springtime Is Guaranteed

H ow hopeless the naked wood of a fruit tree would look to us in February if we had never seen the marvel of springtime!

SOMETIMES THE STATE OF OUR SOULS seems as hopeless as the state of the trees in wintertime. Nothing can possibly be happening, God has forgotten us, the idea of springtime is preposterous.

The naked wood, bare and brittle and dry, is as much a part of the tree's life as the sap's rising in spring. The Lord is still in charge, still moving in mysterious ways even when He gives the enemy of our souls permission to trouble us. Permission was given in the case of Job, a man who in no way deserved the calamities that befell him. He cried out,

Why was I not still-born?
Why did I not die when I came out of the womb?

Why should the sufferer be born to see the light?
Why is life given to men who find it so bitter? (Jb 3:11, 19-20)

To ask why implies a conviction that there *is* a reason somewhere. Somebody must be responsible for this. A scientist, in an essay in *Time*, made a statement unusual nowadays for a scientist: "In the last analysis we are all creationists." A surprising claim in view of the court fights over the teaching of creationism in public schools. Even those who subscribe to the "big bang" theory of the origin of the universe, says the writer, have to admit that something caused the bang. It seems to me there are only two options—the bang was caused or the bang was not caused. To believe the latter is to believe it proceeded by itself from nothing.

Job believed someone was responsible. He addresses God directly:

Can't you take your eyes off me? Won't you leave me alone long enough to swallow my spit? You shaped me and made me; now you've turned to destroy me. You kneaded me like clay, now you're grinding me to a powder.

(Jb 7:19; 10:8-9, my paraphrase)

His friends accuse him of having foolish notions, a bellyful of wind, of being utterly lacking in the fear of God, "pitting himself against the Almighty, charging him head down" (Jb 15:2, 25-26).

Job in turn calls Eliphaz a windbag (16:2), but says his friends (now his enemies) can't hold a candle to God, who "set upon me and mauled me, seized me by the neck and worried me. He set me up as his target; his arrows rained upon me from every side;

pitiless, he cut deep into my vitals, he spilt my gall on the ground" (Jb 16:12-13).

To some of us all this has a familiar ring. We may not be as bold or as eloquent as Job, but we've had feelings akin to his. One of the saddest letters I have ever received was from a man who described himself as skinny and plain, shy and rather "bumbly." But he loves his wife and children, for whom he wants to be the best husband and father God can make him. His letter had the ring of authenticity. It sounded like an earnest and humble man, dead serious about being enlightened and corrected in the plight he describes. He washes dishes and clothes, picks up after everybody, prays with the children at night, gets them ready for school in the morning. He has his own business, and turns over all the money to his wife. He takes her out to dinner, brings her flowers, treats her courteously. But she is nearly unapproachable, says she has no time for kids or housework, prefers her full-time job. She screams at the children until she is hoarse.

"Her temperament has gotten steadily worse. I do whatever I can to avoid upsetting her, and am strengthened only by my commitment to marriage and not by romantic affection. I am undermined. I need to have my serious faults and major defects pointed out to me so that they can be corrected. There must be many, else how could one do so much for so long and not get a loving response?

"I can't change her, only me. But how? The old plow horse simply puts his head down and keeps on going until the job is over. I just don't know what else to do, and I ask the Lord for strength to continue as long as it takes."

Here is an all-too-familiar modern scenario which, to those

ensnared in it, God seems to be overlooking. This man is perplexed, discouraged, almost in despair. But he knows God hasn't forgotten him, and he keeps on praying, seeking God's help and correction.

Note that Job never denies God's existence, never imagines that his troubles come by pure chance. God surely has something to do with it, and he has a thousand questions.

Unknown to Job was a strange encounter that had taken place in the court of heaven. The members, we read, had taken their places in the presence of the Lord, and the Adversary was there among them. The Adversary? In *heaven?* So the Book tells us. God asks him where he has been, and he gives what sounds like a flippant reply: "Ranging over the earth, from end to end." God then calls his attention to a man unique among men, blameless, upright, God-fearing, opposed to evil—the sort of man against whom Satan will surely wish to try his strength.

He takes up the challenge. It's Job, is it? Well of course he's God-fearing. He has every reason to be. God has put him in a special category, with special protection, special privileges and blessings.

"'But stretch out your hand and touch all that he has, and then he will curse you to your face.' Then the Lord said to Satan, 'So be it. All that he has is in your hands; only Job himself you must not touch'" (Jb 1:11-12).

Satan leaves the Lord's presence, and everything Job possesses is taken away—oxen, donkeys, herdsmen, sheep, shepherds, camels, sons, and daughters. Not once in all this did Job sin, or charge God with unreasonableness.

Then came a second scene in the court of heaven, God asking Satan the same question as to his travels and receiving the same answer. He gives a second challenge to the enemy:

❦

Job's integrity remains unshaken. Satan the cynic tosses it back (Jb 2:5, 6): "Stretch out your hand and touch his bone and his flesh, and see if he will not curse you to your face."

"So be it," said the Lord, "He is in your hands; but spare his life."

Job is smitten with running sores, loses his health, his position (he went from the executive suite to an ash heap), and the confidence of his wife. A woman with a thorough-going secular mindset, she advises him to curse God and die.

"If we accept good from God, shall we not accept evil?" says Job, and he "did not utter one sinful word."

Job passes the test. His manifesto is *Though he slay me, yet will I trust him.* Although God answers none of Job's questions, Job is satisfied in the end, for he has seen God, a vision "too wonderful for me to know." The last words we hear from him are, "Therefore I melt away; I repent in dust and ashes" (Jb 42:2-6). Ashes, the place of his torment, become the place of his vision. The vision of God is at the same time the vision of his own abject poverty and ignorance, so the ash heap becomes the place of repentance.

C.S. Lewis defines the problem of suffering in its simplest form: "If God were good, He would wish to make His creatures perfectly happy, and if God were almighty He would be able to do what He wished. But the creatures are not happy. Therefore God lacks either the goodness or the power or both" (*The Problem of Pain*, MacMillan, New York, 1965, p. 14). He goes on to show how the problem is inextricably linked to the mystery of man's free will. Using the metaphor of a game of chess, he writes,

You can deprive yourself of a castle, or allow the other man sometimes to take back a move made inadvertently. But if you conceded everything that at any moment happened to suit him—if all his moves were revocable and if all your pieces disappeared whenever their position on the board was not to his liking—then you could not have a game at all. So it is with the life of souls in a world: fixed laws, consequences unfolding by causal necessity, the whole natural order, are at once the limits within which their common life is confined and also the sole condition under which any such life is possible. Try to exclude the possibility of suffering which the order of nature and the existence of free-wills involves, and you find that you have excluded life itself. *(ibid., p. 22)*

The Book of Job is one of the earliest human records we have, and it is the record of a man confronting evil and confronted by God Himself. A living proof of a living faith was required, not only for Job's friends, but for unseen powers in high places. Job's suffering provided the context for a demonstration of trust. While the patience of Job is often spoken of, he has never impressed me as being particularly patient but he was particularly faithful, even though he had none of the New Testament explanations of suffering (branches must be pruned, thorns are necessary, gold must be refined, we share in the sufferings of Christ, and other reasons, about which more later). To us who have the New Testament, it would seem that Job had very little to go on, yet he kept on talking to God.

Later there was the story of Gideon. Because of Israel's disobedience the Lord had delivered them into the hands of the Midianites who gave them a terrible time for seven years. Then the angel of the Lord came to Gideon, told him the Lord was with him, and called him a brave man. His reply sounds familiar to most of us, I think: if the Lord was with them, why has all this happened and what has become of all those wonderful deeds of His that they have heard so much about from their forebears? It looked to him as though the Lord had cast them off. He hadn't. In fact, the Lord had planned Israel's deliverance, and had chosen Gideon as the deliverer. The man was stunned. *How* could he possibly . . . ?

It's a wonderful story for us timid and faithless ones, for Gideon had no good feelings and no strong self-image to shore him up. He was unsure of himself and even of his lineage, needing reassurance about God, fearful. Happily he did not act on the basis of his misgivings. He obeyed.

Gideon knew nothing of the revelation we have been given in the life and death of the Lord Jesus. How plainly Jesus spoke of the *necessity* of suffering ("in the world you will have trouble," "it was inevitable that Christ should suffer" [Jn 16:33; Lk 24:46, JBP]), and of the importance to the rest of the world of living proof ("The Prince of this world approaches. He has no rights over me; but the world must be shown that I love the Father, and do exactly as he commands" [Jn 14:30-31]).

We may take heart from the suffering of Job. Suffering was the necessary proof of the reality of his faith—to us, as to his contemporaries and his enemy Satan (his and ours). The suffering of our Savior proved the reality of His love for His Father. The world still needs to be shown that there are those who, no matter what the circumstances, will, for love of Him, do exactly what God commands. The end He has in view is a glorious one. We can fully count on that, as we can count on the naked wood's one day exploding into a glory of blossom.

❧

SEVEN

Blessed Inconveniences

he flowers that are bent on perfecting them-selves, by becoming double, are sure to end in barrenness. . . . The true ideal flower is the one that uses its gifts as a means to an end. The brightness and sweetness are not for its own glory; they are but to attract the bees and butterflies that will fertilize and make it fruitful.

ST. AUGUSTINE IN HIS *CONFESSIONS* describes in intimate detail his own conflicts of soul, vacillating between good and evil, longing for eternal delights while held down by temporal lusts. He could not desire either one thing or the other with his whole heart. Soul-sick, tormented, accusing himself, "rent asunder with grievous perplexities . . . rolling and turning me in my chain. And Thou, O Lord, pressedst upon me in my inward parts by a severe mercy, redoubling the lashes of fear and shame." He pours out his heart in thanksgiving to God for those "lashes" of many kinds, needful to save him from himself. Thanksgiving for lashes? Who can be grateful for pain? Only those who see beyond to the ineffable mercy, tender and severe, which is silently at work.

The word *suffering* is much too grand to apply to most of our troubles, but if we don't learn to refer the little things to God how shall we learn to refer the big ones? A definition which covers all sorts of trouble, great or small, is this: *having what you don't want, or wanting what you don't have.*

The vicissitudes of travel furnish plenty of what Janet Erskine Stuart calls "blessed inconveniences," occasions which fit both categories in our definition.

My husband Lars and I were on our way home from Madison, Wisconsin, with a change of planes in Chicago. We had an hour's layover, so I sat down, as is my wont, and let Lars take care of everything. He has a way with people, and although we had boarding passes, he went to the counter, as is his wont, to check our seats and to find out if the flight was a full one. Sometimes when it isn't he gets better seats. When the flight was called I put away my book and followed Lars in blind trust.

"They tell me the plane is half-empty," he said, "so we can take any seats we like." Tickets were taken, boarding passes inspected, and down the jetway we went. Funny—the plane was full. Even our seats were taken. We checked our seat numbers again, the people in our seats checked theirs. Another case of double booking, which we reported to the stewardess. She examined all boarding passes and found no explanation. Finally she found two seats, not together. Kind passengers offered to switch, so we settled in together, buckled our seat belts, and heard the door thud shut. The captain's voice announced, "Our flying time to Spokane will be three hours." I jerked to attention.

"Spokane?" I said to the man on my left. "Did he say *Spokane?*"

"Sure did. Where did you think you were going?"

Imagine the alacrity with which we leaped out of our seats, grabbed our hand baggage, and rushed forward. Imagine also our embarrassment and the disgust of the three hundred-plus passengers whose plane was held up for a full fifteen minutes before the jetway was reconnected and the door could be opened to let us off. We were thankful the plane had not been on the runway when we heard the announcement. The Boston plane, however, had left at 6:55, as scheduled, with our baggage aboard, not to mention a special seafood meal Lars had ordered which he was sorry to miss.

"Oh well," said Lars as we headed back into the terminal, "We can catch the 8:55."

"Hmm," I thought to myself. "How does he know there's an 8:55?" I am learning not to ask too many questions, however. I find it isn't necessary, it doesn't make for peace, and Lars almost always knows what he's doing.

I sat down with my book. He went to the counter, returned with the word that he had booked us on the 8:55. There would be no dinner on that one, so we found a fast food joint and ate a styrofoam plate of nearly unidentifiable food, listed on the menu as Chinese. Strolling leisurely back toward the gate, I checked the monitor, wanting to make sure we were on our way to the right gate this time. There it was: Boston, flight number whatever, 8:25, DEPARTED.

I searched frantically for the 8:55. There was no such flight. What ever made him think there was? We stared at each other, jaws agape. I thought of a few nasty remarks I might make to my husband, decided against it, and then we both burst out laughing. Back to the counter went Lars.

"Sorry, sir. The 8:25 was the last flight to Boston tonight."

"How about on another carrier?"

"No, last flight on any carrier."

We found a hotel and flew home early the next morning.

The story is amusing—from a distance. But it had been a rather rigorous weekend and we were both very tired, very eager to get home. Suffering? Of course it wasn't that, not in the usual sense of the word. Trouble? It was that. We wanted what we didn't have—a flight home. We had what we didn't want—a night in Chicago without luggage.

Why?

Irene Webster-Smith, missionary to Japan, took as her life verse three words from Philippians 4:6, "Everything by prayer." I am trying to make this the habit of my life, no matter whether the thing looks big or small, so while Lars was making phone calls to find us a room I was asking God what He had in this for me to learn. He reminded me of a line in the Orthodox prayer I use regularly: "Teach me to treat all that comes to me with peace of soul and with firm conviction that Your will governs all. In unforeseen events let me not forget that all are sent by You."

Had He not answered that prayer in that moment as we stood under the monitor? He *was* teaching me. He *had* given me peace of soul. He had not let me forget that He had something to do with the whole thing. He reminded me that it was not for nothing. Of course I wanted to know exactly what it *was* for, but there were no explanations. Weeks later He granted me just a tiny glimpse of a part of His purpose. I told the story to a group, and a young woman said to me afterwards, "I know why you missed two planes in a row. I put myself in your place, and I *knew* I would have been furious with my husband. God spoke to me about that. He also reminded me how stupid it is to lash out when somebody has made a mistake—after all, *nobody* would do a thing like that *on purpose.*"

There is a subtle snare in self-improvement programs. We may easily be like the flowers Lilias Trotter describes, bent on perfecting themselves, and by becoming double, ending in barrenness. We cannot make ourselves holy. But when we surrender ourselves to the Lord, learning day by day to treat all that comes to us with peace of soul and firm conviction that His will governs *all,* He will see to our growth in grace. He will so govern the events in our lives, down to the smallest detail, as to provide for us the conditions which may make us fruitful. It is not for our sake but for the sake of others. The beauty of the flower is not for itself. It offers itself to God's sunshine and rain, gives its fragrance to any who pass by, but it must wither and die before the fruit can be produced.

It awes me to see this principle at work. It was a very small "death" for me to die there in O'Hare Airport. It was a very great grace that God should use it later to help one woman.

Faith need never ask, "But what good did this do *me?*" Faith already knows that *everything* that happens fits into a pattern for good to those who love God. An inconvenience is always, whether we see it or not, a *blessed* inconvenience. We may rest in the promise that God is fitting together a good many more things than are any of our business. We need never *see* "what

EIGHT

Even the Fair Petals Must Fall

he principle [of the cross] is pictured in the plant. As it develops there comes a fresh stage of yielding. At first it was only the dead, disfigured leaves that had to go. Now it is the fair new petals. They must fall, and for no visible reason—no one seems enriched by this stripping.

A YOUNG MOTHER CALLED TO ASK FOR "something that will help me to trust in the Lord." She explained that she has several small children, she herself is thirty years old, and she has cancer. Chemotherapy has done its hideous work of making her totally bald. The prognosis is not good. Could I say to her, "Don't worry. God will heal you?" I could not.

When Jesus was speaking with His disciples before His crucifixion, He gave them His parting gift: peace such as the world can never give. Is that gift not for us also? Could I perhaps show her this?

"Set your troubled hearts at rest and banish your fears," He went on to say—but not because nothing "bad" would happen. He knew exactly what He was about to endure. "I shall not talk much longer with you, for the Prince of this world approaches. He has no rights over me; but the world must be shown that I love the Father, and do exactly as He commands" (Jn 14:27, 30-31).

The peace of the Lord was not contingent upon His escaping death. I could not promise this dear woman physical healing. I could, however, remind her that He would never let go of her, that His love enfolded her and her precious children every minute of every day and every night, and that underneath are the Everlasting Arms.

But is that enough? Was I serving up mere platitudes? Think of the "stripping" she was facing—not only the loss of her beauty but of her health, her powers, perhaps her life, which would mean a terrible stripping of her children. Who was to be enriched by this?

The disciples' worst fears were about to be realized, yet Jesus commanded (yes, *commanded*) them to be at peace. All would be well, all manner of things would be well—in the end. In a short time, however, the prince of this world was to have his hour of power. Not that Satan had any *rights* over Jesus. Far from it. Nor has he *rights* over any of God's children. But it has to be proven from time to time (to the underworld, as in Job's case, as well as to this world) that there is such a thing as obedient faith, faith which is not dependent on receiving benefits only. Jesus had to show the world that He loved the Father and would, no matter what happened, do what He said.

Was my caller comforted and helped by realizing that Jesus had been over the course, that He would lead her through no darker rooms than He went through before? I don't know. Did I answer her plea for something that would help her to trust Him? I hope so. I prayed that the Comforter Himself would speak to her, and as I lay in bed that night I went over in my mind the things that have transfigured my own thinking, things learned very slowly, very imperfectly, and over many years.

Suffering was indispensable for the world's salvation.

There was no other way but the cross.

The servant is not greater than his Lord.

If we suffer with Him we shall also reign with Him.

Shall we not follow the Master in suffering as in everything else, sharing with Him in His work, that the world and the devils themselves may be shown in this last decade of the millennium that we love the Father and will do just what He says? The world does not want to be *told.* The world must be *shown*—shown the very guts of faith.

Does our faith rest on having prayers answered as we think they should be answered, or does it rest on that mighty love that went down into death for us? We can't really tell where it rests, can we, until we're in real trouble. I prayed for that mother, prayed of course for healing of the cancer (we are told to make our requests known to God), but prayed above all for her peace. In His will alone, as Dante wrote, is our peace.

"True, he died on the cross in weakness, but he lives by the power of God; and we who share his weakness shall by the power of God live with him in your service" (2 Cor 13:4).

Staggering promise, realized only in the cross. We in our miseries may share His weakness, and therefore live with Him in the service of others.

All that is given is meant to be poured forth. The flower

pours forth its sweetness, the tree its blossom and fruit, its powers of purification, its shade, its wood. In the words of Ugo Bassi, "Measure thy life by loss and not by gain; not by the wine drunk but by the wine poured forth, for love's strength standeth in love's sacrifice, and he that suffereth most hath most to give." Bassi was another of those whose words ministered to Lilias Trotter. She made them the caption for her watercolor of the dandelion seed-globe, which has "long ago surrendered its golden petals, and has reached its crowning stage of dying—the delicate seed-globe must break up now—it gives and gives until it has nothing left."

The story of Joseph, so rich with spiritual instruction for all of us, shows Bassi's principle. Joseph suffered much for many long years at the hands of evil people, and through those hard years of being hated by his brothers, sold into slavery, lied about and imprisoned, he was faithful. The outcome of what must have seemed senseless suffering when he was in the midst of it was that he had much to give. Through the sovereign working of God behind the scenes, he gained a position of power which enabled him to save the lives of his father and brothers. "He that suffereth most hath most to give." He could not in any other way have had it to give.

Haven't we seen this demonstrated time and again in our own experience? Those who speak most deeply to our hearts in times of trouble are invariably those who have suffered. They have much to give. We recognize its authenticity and willingly receive it. They testify to the truth of Solomon's wisdom, "He who refreshes others will himself be refreshed" (Prv 11:25). So the cycle continues—love's sacrifice (not only of the disfigured leaves, but even of the fair, new petals), then the fruit of that sacrifice in the blessing of others, and that blessing rebounding to the refreshment of the one who sacrificed. "If a man will let himself be lost for my sake, that man is safe" (Lk 9:24).

The sacrifice we speak of here ought not to be a morbid and gloomy sort of thing, with emphasis on our losses and deprivations, but a glad offering of love. A friend told me she had seen her husband's travel as her own inconvenience and suffering, but now was learning to make it an offering of love.

Lilias Trotter had to face the misunderstanding of friends and family in turning her back on things they valued highly, but she learned that there was not only the pain of renunciation but sweetness and peace, "the bliss of a yielded heart."

"You can only obey God," she wrote to a friend who faced the breaking of human ties to follow Christ. "Let us give ourselves away to Him for His world—away down to the deepest depths of our being, time, influence—and home if He calls us to it; but our heart of hearts first. Separation has nothing austere or narrow about it when it is unto Him. To bear His Name with all that is wrapped up in it of fragrance and healing and power, to enter into His life and share His eternal purpose, is a calling for which it is well worth counting all things but loss" (I.R. Govan Stewart: *The Love That Was Stronger*, p. 19).

We are not often called to great sacrifice, but daily we are presented with the chance to make small ones—a chance to make someone cheerful, a chance to do some small thing to make someone comfortable or contented, a chance to lay down our petty preferences or cherished plans. This probably requires us to relinquish something—our own convenience or comfort, our own free evening, our warm fireside, or even our habitual shyness or reserve or pride. My liberty must be

NINE

Open Hands

ee the flower in maturity. The calyx hands have unclasped utterly now. They have folded themselves back, past all power of closing again upon the petals, leaving the golden crown free to float away when God's time and wind come.

OPEN HANDS SHOULD CHARACTERIZE THE SOUL'S attitude toward God—open to receive what He wants to give, open to give back what He wants to take. Acceptance of the will of God means relinquishment of our own. If our hands are full of our own plans, there isn't room to receive His.

The outer leaves of a flower make up what is called the calyx. Like tiny hands it clasps the bud, holding tightly to the furled petals, but as the flower develops the hold is loosened, though still maintaining the power to contract. In maturity there is a complete release, a letting go, and the mini-hands are folded back, past all power of closing.

I have been reading the letters of Joan Andrews, a woman willing literally to renounce her rights and her liberty for the sake of the liberation of others—those smallest, most helpless and voiceless ones, the preborn. She serves the pro-life cause by her willingness to be treated as the unborn are treated, rejected as they are rejected. For her unbreakable passive resistance she was arrested more than one hundred twenty times, and finally sentenced to five years, most of it in solitary confinement. Her letters describe prison conditions, from the almost continuous screaming and cursing, the homosexual activity and the mental breakdowns that occur, to so small a thing as not being allowed to write a letter with a pen.

"I hate writing with a pencil. One of the inmates here who did some time at Broward said that inmates there were permitted to use pens. I can't wait to get there. Never thought something so little would mean so much."

In her reflections on non-cooperation, written when she entered Broward Correctional in November, 1986, she writes,

"We must see a . . . distinction between the idea of a stand taken as witness that rejects cooperation with a system of evil—for example the court sentencing prolifers to punish them for rescuing babies, and to discourage others from doing likewise . . . and the spiritual, inner attitude and demeanor of the sentenced rescuer who does thank God joyfully for the privilege to suffer in His name and endure injustice for the sake of the more grievously offended preborn. By our love and humility and gentleness this attitude of accepting injustice upon oneself for Christ will shine through to others even while we noncooperate in prison. We 'noncooperate' in love. In this way, for purposes of witness, of example, of purification, and thereby far from taking an easier road, we join ourselves more closely to the preborn who are abandoned by society" (*You Reject Them, You Reject Me*, edited by Richard Cowden

❧

Guido, Trinity Communications, Manassas, Virginia, 1988, pp. 104f).

Joan Andrews is an example to me of the cost of an utter "unclasping" of one's own rights and privileges. The call—*Will you do this one thing for Me?*—comes to each of us in some form. The thing required may be severely criticized, as Joan's stance has been.

Often the things which are taking place in the spiritual life are hidden to all but the eye of God, while the outward appearance seems nothing but unnecessary waste. The judge who imposed Joan Andrews's sentence said, "It's a shame Miss Andrews has chosen to waste her life in prison instead of accomplishing something." He could not fathom her regarding it as a privilege, as the apostles also did, to suffer shame for the name of Christ. Paul even called it a happiness. Joan had not chosen to waste her life but to spend it for her Master—a very different thing, frequently misinterpreted. She unclasped her hands utterly, "past all power of closing again," and there she sits in her cell, praying, singing, writing her letters, encouraging and ministering to other prisoners (even in solitary she was able to read the Bible to the girl in the next cell).

This is what it means to be a witness—to live the life of sacrificial love, a life which makes no sense whatsoever if this world is all there is.

We used to have a magnolia (also called a tulip) tree on our front lawn. The velvety buds would be there all winter and suddenly, one spring day, they would burst into bloom. There was not a leaf on the tree, only hundreds of lovely, tall, pink and white, tulip-shaped cups. I drank in its beauty from the window of my study, knowing that it would be very short-lived. In two or three days the green lawn would be littered with pink scraps. The tree had loosed them, taken *hands off*.

Why this waste?

Why this sacrifice?

Why *this*, when things seemed so promising?

Often there seems to be no visible reason for our having to let go. But life, our spiritual life in Christ, depends on it. The life-out-of-death cycle must proceed.

There are many voices to advocate escape from suffering through drugs, divorce, abortion, euthanasia, suicide. "How far we are," writes a friend of mine, "from saying with St. Paul, 'All I care for is to know Christ, to experience the power of his resurrection (no problem there) and to share his sufferings, in growing conformity with his death'" (Phil 3:10).

Eternal life means knowing God. All our life on earth is designed to facilitate that. But knowing Him must include sharing His sufferings by *reproducing the pattern of His death*. Instead of seeking first for escape from suffering, the soul hungry to know Christ will seek *in* it the means to know Him better. Our human nature would look first for someone to blame, and focus its responses on that person. The spiritual mind looks first to God, "Teach me Thy way." The rest can wait.

We are not told that we must go out looking for suffering. It will come in God's time, in the measure He metes out. We must hear the call (He calls His sheep by name) and we must answer, even if it means taking a solitary way, misunderstood and even scorned by others of the same flock. We will then find our chance to know Him, to reproduce the pattern as He relinquished His hold on all that was His, emptied Himself to share our lives, came to earth where even His own did not

🌿

receive Him, and was finally obedient even to the point of death.

Why *this* waste—of His perfectly pure life?

So that through death he might break the power of him who had death at his command, that is, the devil; and might liberate those who, through fear of death, had all their lifetime been in servitude. It is not angels, mark you, that he takes to himself, but the sons of Abraham. And therefore he had to be made like these brothers of his in every way, so that he might be merciful and faithful as their high priest before God, to expiate the sins of the people. For since he himself has passed through the test of suffering, he is able to help those who are meeting their test now.   (Heb 2:14-18)

Whatever today's test may be, through accident, physical disability, our own mistakes or failures or disobedience, perhaps the hostility of others, He is able to help us meet our test. He was made like us. He had to be, in order to die. He had to die in order to break death's power. His was a surrender, not to a fate He could not avoid, but to His Father. When we open our lives to the will of the Father, we enter into that same mystery. It is true that Jesus was put into the hands of evil men. There are times when following Him means just that, as it has in a radical and costly way for Daniel and Paul and Dietrich Bonhoeffer and Corrie Ten Boom and Betty Scott Stam and Joan Andrews and numberless others in the history of the church who have been imprisoned or killed for their faith. It is not the external circumstances themselves that enable us to reproduce the pattern of His death, but our willingness to accept the circumstances for His sake.

Relinquishment is always a part of the process of maturing. When Christian parents have done all that can be done to shape their children for God, the time comes when the hands must let go. The child, now a responsible adult, must be released. For any parent this is painful, even when the child is moving in the direction the parents prayed for. The child's continued development, and the spiritual health of the parents as well, depend on the willingness to accept this next stage of the cycle—hands off, ready to part without a struggle, giving up authority and control, entrusting that child to God.

When, on the other hand, the child has obviously rejected what the parents have taught, the severing is painful in the extreme. All has been done that could be done and all has been done in vain. Nevertheless the time comes to let go, as it came for the father of the prodigal when he turned his wayward son over to God. He must have foreseen the direction he would take, but he prayed for him and waited every day for his return. God cared for that young man as the father could never have done, brought him to bankruptcy (another severe mercy), and returned him to his father, repentant and willing even to be a mere servant.

It is a merciful Father who strips us when we need to be stripped, as the tree needs to be stripped of its blossoms. He is not finished with us yet, whatever the loss we suffer, for as we loose our hold on visible things, the invisible become more precious—where our treasure is, there will our hearts be.

He may be asking us to sell a much-loved house, to part with material things we no longer need (someone else may need them), to retire from a position in which we feel ourselves irreplaceable, to turn over to Him fears which hold us in bondage, forms of self-improvement or recreation or social life which hinder obedience.

"Does all this seem hard?" asks Lilias Trotter, "Does any soul, young in physical or in spiritual life, shrink back and say, 'I would rather remain in the springtime—I do not want to reach unto the things that are before if it means all this matter of pain and dying.'

"To such comes the Master's voice, 'Fear none of those things which thou shalt suffer' (Rv 2:10, AV). You are right to be glad in His April days while He gives them. Every stage of the heavenly growth in us is lovely to Him; He is the God of the daisies and the lambs and the merry child hearts!"

TEN

Hour of Desolation

ave faith, like the flowers to let the old things go. Adorn His beatitude, His "blessed is he, whosoever shall not be offended in Me"—the beatitude of the trusting—even if you have to appropriate it like John the Baptist in an hour of desolation.

IMAGINE A WORLD IN WHICH NOBODY had anything he didn't want—no toothaches, taxes, touchy relatives, traffic jams.

Now imagine a world in which everybody had everything they wanted—perfect weather, perfect marriage, perfect health, perfect score, perfect happiness, with money and power to boot.

The world we live in, however, is full of good things we can't have and bad things we don't want, much worse things than toothaches and traffic jams—war, famine, drought, floods, volcanoes, cancer, AIDS. One week I kept track of the tales of sorrow that came to me in that week's mail alone: desertion, death, disease, divorce, depression, alcoholism, addiction, abuse, homosexuality, and suicide. Hardly a day closes without news of a broken marriage or broken health for someone we know.

"Supposing you eliminated suffering," wrote Malcolm Muggeridge, "what a dreadful place the world would be! because everything that corrects the tendency of man to feel over-important and over-pleased with himself would disappear. He's bad enough now, but he would be absolutely intolerable if he never suffered."

Although the Book of Job settles the question of whether man's suffering is always punishment for evil—it isn't, since God Himself called Job a blameless man—we must not overlook the punitive aspect of suffering. Sometimes we do need chastisement. Suffering gives us occasion to examine ourselves, adjust our priorities, reset our sights, and confess our sins. It is a discipline, administered by a loving heavenly Father who "lays the rod on every son whom he acknowledges. . . . If you escape the discipline in which all sons share, you must be bastards and no true sons. . . . Discipline, no doubt, is never pleasant; at the time it seems painful, but in the end it yields for those who have been trained by it the peaceful harvest of an honest life" (Heb 12:6, 8, 11).

St. Augustine recounts how his mother, when a young girl, acquired the habit of tasting wine when she was sent by her parents to draw some from the hogshead. This was not out of any desire to drink, but merely a "mirthful freak" which sprang from the exuberance of her youth. Day by day she would taste a bit more until she was drinking a little cup brimful.

"What didst Thou then, O my God?" writes Augustine, "How didst Thou cure her? how heal her? didst Thou not out of another soul bring forth a hard and a sharp taunt, like a lancet out of Thy secret store, and with one touch remove all that foul stuff?"

God's "lancet" was the bitter insult of a maidservant who caught Monica tasting the wine and called her a wine-bibber. "With which taunt she, stung to the quick, saw the foulness of her fault, and instantly condemned and forsook it. As flattering friends pervert, so reproachful enemies mostly correct. . . . For she in her anger sought to vex her young mistress, not to amend her. . . . But Thou, Lord, Governor of all in heaven and earth, who turnest to Thy purposes the deepest currents, and the ruled turbulence of the tide of times, didst by the unhealthiness of one soul, heal another."

Suffering creates the possibility of growth in holiness, but only to those who, by letting all else go, are open to the training—not by arguing with the Lord about what they did or did not do to deserve punishment, but by praying, "Lord, show me what You have for me in this."

The apostle Paul, a holy man, needed his thorn. He says so himself, "to keep me from becoming unduly elated by the magnificence" (2 Cor 12:7) of certain extraordinary visions and revelations granted him. He was in danger of spiritual pride, a deadly sin, and, understanding that God was sparing him this, he was not offended. He could have been, if he were not as in tune with his Lord as he obviously was. He could have been very angry at the sudden comedown—God had given him spiritual revelations and then zapped him with sharp physical pain. Instead, his spirit was one of humility and teachableness.

Referring to trouble that had come upon him and his companions in the province of Asia (note that it was when they were faithfully doing God's work) Paul writes, "The burden of it was far too heavy for us to bear, so heavy that we even despaired of life. Indeed, we felt in our hearts that we had received a death-sentence." Does he charge God with injustice? No. He has learned something: "This was meant to teach us not to place reliance on ourselves, but on God who raises the dead" (2 Cor 1:8-9).

Suffering is meant for correction of the sufferer himself. Did the great apostle need correction? Of course he did. He was tempted like the rest of us to place reliance on himself.

Suffering is also meant to help somebody else. Like all gifts, the gift of suffering is not for ourselves alone, but for the sake of the body of Christ. "Indeed, it is for your sake that all things are ordered, so that, as the abounding grace of God is shared by more and more, the greater may be the chorus of thanksgiving that ascends to the glory of God" (2 Cor 4:15).

While Amy Carmichael, an Irish missionary to India, endured almost constant pain for the last twenty years of her life, she was confined to her room and mostly to bed. But during those years she wrote more than twenty books, books which I doubt she could have written if she had not been physically incapacitated. She would not have had time, for one thing. Beyond that, those books were unquestionably the very fruits of her suffering. One of them, *Rose from Brier*, was a book of letters to the ill.

She writes in her introduction, "Reading them through I am troubled to find them so personal and sometimes so intimate. It is not that I think the personal or the intimate interesting or valuable [oh that she *had* thought so—she might have given us even more!], but that I did not know how to give the comfort wherewith we ourselves are comforted without giving something of my own soul also. If I had waited till the harrow had lifted, perhaps a less tired mind would have found a better way. But then the book would have been from the *well* to the ill, and not from the *ill* to the ill, which I think is what it is meant to be—a rose plucked straight from a brier."

She did not know then that the "harrow" would never be lifted. If she had waited for that we would not have had the comfort and consolation which overflowed for us. It is good to have a twentieth-century affirmation of what Paul had discovered in the first century:

> Praise be to the God and Father of our Lord Jesus Christ, the all-merciful Father, the God whose consolation never fails us! He comforts us in all our troubles, so that we in turn may be able to comfort others in any trouble of theirs and to share with them the consolation we ourselves receive from God. As Christ's cup of suffering overflows, and we suffer with him, so also through Christ our consolation overflows. If distress be our lot, it is the price we pay for your consolation, for your salvation; if our lot be consolation, it is to help us to bring you comfort, and strength to face with fortitude the same sufferings we now endure. And our hope for you is firmly grounded; for we know that if you have part in the suffering, you have part also in the divine consolation.
>
> (2 Cor 1:3-7)

There is a fellowship among those who suffer, for they live in a world separated from the rest of us. When my husband Addison Leitch was dying of cancer he felt keenly the impossibility of my understanding his experience. "It's two different worlds we're living in," he said, "and there's no commerce between the two." He could not help feeling that I did not care enough. I cared as much as a wife can care for a husband she adores and cannot bear to lose, but it was not enough. I did not know what Add knew. I had not been there. When we went to the waiting room of the radiation department at the hospital, however, we met others who *knew*—a little bald boy with red X's on his temples, a man whose lower jaw had been removed, a police woman who was taking radiation without her husband's knowledge, for he was paralyzed at home and "I can't tell him my cancer's back—he'd die if he knew."

There is a much deeper fellowship into which the Christian who suffers may enter. It is the fellowship of Christ's suffering. Christ's cup of suffering overflows *and we suffer with Him.*

John the Baptist had to appropriate in his lonely prison cell the lesson of the flower's letting everything go. It was the hour of his desolation, but he was not offended, he was blessed, which means in modern English, *happy.* May the "beatitude of trusting" be ours as well, even in such an hour.

ELEVEN

Nothing to Lose

he one vital thing is to keep obedient in spirit, then you will be ready to let the flowertime pass if He bids you, when the sun of His love has worked some more ripening. You will feel by then that to try to keep the withering blossoms would be to cramp and cripple your soul. It is loss to keep when God says, "Give."

ONE OF THE GREAT BLESSINGS of my life is the privilege of meeting and corresponding with a variety of holy people. (With this privilege goes a greater responsibility—much given, therefore much required.) In an exchange of letters with a Carmelite nun I raised the question of self-image, confessing that I could not help feeling at times a bit envious of her and her sisters because of their complete freedom from having to give any thought at all to hairdos, makeup, or what to wear when. What a huge chunk of time those things take.

"I'm afraid concerns with self-image can still all too easily take other forms," she wrote. "Especially where we live so close to one another, we can make ourselves very dependent on the

🦋

frowns or smiles or raised eyebrows of those we live with. I don't think the temptation is to try to impress so much as it might be to act with an eye to image in the sense of 'Lest they think . . .' Isn't it true that the chains that bind us are often those we forge for ourselves?

"It is precisely because we have received the Spirit that we can experience our bondage as bondage as we groan for the full freedom of the sons of God. Surely that is reason enough for joy. And such hope, just knowing the Spirit Himself is pleading for us!"

Our Lord Jesus was a man wholly free from thoughts of Himself and His own reputation. The Pharisees recognized that clearly. "Master," they said, "you are an honest man, we know; you teach in all honesty the way of life that God requires, truckling to no man, whoever he may be" (Mt 22:16). His purpose was pure because His love was pure. We whose purpose is a mixture and whose love is far from pure, cannot bear criticism, disagreement, or anything that might sully the reputation we hope we have built up. This is bondage—of our own making. It cramps and cripples our souls. Why not open our hands and give it all over?

The gateway that leads out into life is small. We can't get through it with the baggage of pride. Only the humble enter. They do so by the willingness to stoop, to accept weaknesses and sorrows and deaths. The gateway opens to new powers, new joys, new Life, where they find a "grand new independence of any earthly thing to satisfy, the liberty of those who have nothing to lose because they have nothing to keep" (Trotter: *Parables of the Cross*).

When close friends misunderstood a decision a woman had made and judged her to be making use of money not rightly

🌱

hers, she spent some sleepless hours at night and was much distracted in her prayers over this matter, keenly desiring to vindicate herself. Then she saw the cross as her "safe and happy shelter," and laid at its foot

- — her care for her reputation,
- — the impression she had made,
- — her desire to be vindicated,
- — her longing for justice,
- — her disquiet at the dilemma in which others had been put,
- — her hurt and theirs,
- — her impatience—wanting a solution NOW.

This renunciation freed her. She had nothing to lose because she had nothing to keep.

Another woman wrote of how God had taught her to let go. She and her husband agreed that she should give up her job in order to mother the children.

"When I quit work our income was cut practically in half. We felt then that it was a good possibility that we would have to give up our home. Well, we're at that point now. We sure haven't gotten *any* encouragement or positive reinforcement from most of our friends and relatives. Some of them think we have lost our minds. But we have decided that it's more important for me to be at home with my son who is five now, and the one due in a month, than to stay and strain just to keep a 'nice' house. I would have to continue my job and always worry about where the money for the mortgage was coming from. It's just not worth that. I'm ready to be a wife and a mother full-time, not part-time.

"But we're going through such 'withdrawal' ourselves because of leaving this house! It's *harder* than I thought it would be. It's hard to let go of these worldly things, no matter how 'spiritual' we think we are. I'm just so aware of how God is stripping away things that I thought were so important. I gave up *my* name (seven years after I was married!), I gave up my career, now my home. But I'm *beginning* to see God's sufficiency. It's easy to say sometimes, but when He really pulls the rug out from under you, what do you have left to stand on? . . . God is taking me through this intense breaking process. Just when I think I can't handle any more, He adds more. A friend said God must think I am strong to handle all this, or He wouldn't be doing it. I guess He *always* knows better than we do. . . ."

The writer of this letter had talked with one of her friends about the situation, and the friend had asked her if she knew the Lord any better now.

"How true! That's what we're supposed to be doing while we're here, isn't it?" she wrote to me.

That's it exactly. Because hers is an obedient spirit she is learning to know Him in the fellowship of His suffering, and she is experiencing in the process something of the power of His resurrection—"I'm *beginning* to see His sufficiency."

Without these hard realities could she have begun? God gave the hard realities that He might give the hard lesson. In her struggles Christ Himself suffers, for we are His body. It is in *this* dimension that we suffer with Him and He with us—that we compose His body.

"God has combined the various parts of the body . . . so that there might be no sense of division in the body, but that all its organs might feel the same concern for one another. If one organ suffers, they all suffer together. . . . Now you are Christ's body, and each of you a limb or organ of it" (1 Cor 12:24-27).

🌱

Each time God gives us a hard lesson He desires also to give us Himself. If we open our hands to receive the lesson we open our hearts to receive *Him*, and with Himself His vision to see the glory in the surrender, whether of small things like self-esteem and reputation, or bigger things like a career and a home. He has been over the trail first, for He surrendered His glory, His equality with the Father, His omnipotence, His omnipresence, His *all*, when He came into our world. He stands ready today to supply us with His wisdom to understand what He wants to teach, and His strength to carry through, for He never allows us to undergo anything for which He has not promised the strength to endure. His commands are always accompanied by power to obey. The Everlasting Arms are always underneath us, the everlasting love always surrounds us.

A naval officer once wrote to his wife, "If you should hear that our cruiser was sunk and none were saved, then do not weep. The sea in which my body sinks is nothing but the hollow of my Savior's hand, and nothing can snatch me from it."

TWELVE

The Songs of Suffering

bserve the expression of abandonment about the wild rose calyx as time goes on, and it begins to grow towards the end for which it has had to count all things but loss. The look of dumb emptiness has gone. It is flung back joyously now, for simultaneously with the new dying a richer life has begun to work at its heart—so much death, so much life.

GOD'S ULTIMATE PURPOSE in all suffering is joy. Scripture is full of songs of praise that came out of great trials. The feast of the Passover commemorated God's deliverance from the long slavery Israel had endured in Egypt. The last day of the Passover was to be a pilgrim feast, according to God's command, so that they could tell their sons what God had done for them when He brought them out of Egypt. The sacrifice of the firstborn male of every animal and the redemption of every firstborn son were signs of this great delivery, sacrifices of thanksgiving.

When God miraculously saved His people from the chariots

of the army of Egypt by driving back the sea all night with a strong east wind, the people put their faith in Him and in His servant Moses, and all sang a song together.

> I will sing to the Lord, for he has risen up in triumph;
> the horse and his rider he has hurled into the sea.
>> The Lord is my refuge and my defence,
>> he has shown himself my deliverer.
>> He is my God, and I will glorify him.   (Ex 15:1-2)

The song goes on for pages, recounting the Lord's marvelous power, love, and mercy. Miriam the prophetess took up a tambourine and the women danced while Miriam sang. The greater the peril they had been in, the greater the joy of deliverance.

The terrors and privations of their long journey through the wilderness had to be endured, but how much more wonderful the promised land would be as a result. Who can enjoy the fire who has never been cold, or cold water who has never been thirsty?

The heartbreak of the prodigal's father turned into dancing, singing, and feasting when the son came home.

The angels in heaven sing more joyfully over the repentance of a single sinner than over ninety-nine who need no repentance.

The woman who loses a small coin is so ecstatic to find it that she calls in her friends to rejoice with her.

And the virgin Mary, a humble village girl, sings her Magnificat:

> "Tell out, my soul, the greatness of the Lord, rejoice, rejoice, my spirit, in God my Savior; so tenderly has he looked upon

his servant,
     humble as she is. . . ."   (Lk 1:46-48)

I read a little story by a priest who suffers from tinnitus, an incurable and very annoying buzzing in the ears. Because he believes that we are responsible for our own happiness, he has elected to regard this "little problem," as he calls it, as an opportunity rather than a curse.

"Waking up in the morning to the sound of a thousand crickets is not pleasant. Thank God, during the day I'm busy and I seldom advert to it, but the din never stops."

Instead of offering canned advice to others he simply tells how he crossed over from a frantic search for relief to a relatively calm condition of acceptance. He believes that the greatest honor he can give to God is to live gladly because of the knowledge of His love. His happiness he regards as a sign of gratitude to God, so nothing must spoil it; therefore he thinks of tinnitus as a friend, not an enemy. He pretends that the shrill sound in his head is an echo of the song of the universe, as all the earth blesses the Lord—the birds, the rivers, the howling winds.

"I let the buzzing in my ears become my unceasing prayer of praise. 'Cry out with joy to the Lord, all the earth. Serve the Lord with gladness. Come before him, singing for joy.'"

It isn't the problems that determine our destiny. It's how we respond.

The knowledge also that our sufferings are taken up into Christ's is a source of joy. Indeed, the thought of His cross and what it did for me is in times of deep sorrow the only *pure* joy I can know. We may not feel like shaking tambourines and dancing when we are nailed to a bed by pain. Yet the pain itself

may become an offering when we know that we are allowed to
help to complete, in our poor human flesh, "the full tale of
Christ's afflictions still to be endured, for the sake of his body
which is the church" (Col 1:24). It is *Christ in us* that makes
this possible. Once we have opened ourselves to grace, then
Christ Himself takes up His dwelling in us. If we suffer, He
suffers. We *are* His body here on earth. This poor human flesh,
yours and mine, is where Jesus now lives, so pain bestows on us
the incomprehensible privilege of helping to carry to comple-
tion the quota He must endure. As we accept this burden with
thankfulness, we enter into an ever-deepening fellowship of
His sufferings—but let us never forget that it was His own
perfect and complete sacrifice of Himself that opened to us this
possibility. Because of *that* we become His dwelling place.
Ought not this to make us glad? Isn't this reason enough to
make our sufferings a sacrifice of praise?

No matter how far along our spiritual pilgrimage we may
have come, we need to be shown again and again that humble,
ordinary things can be very holy and very full of God. They are
not "religious" things, they are plain, earthly things. We may
hope for visions and revelations and "wonderful experiences,"
forgetting that the context of the revelation of God to each of
His children is *exactly where that one is,* here, on earth, in this
house, this kitchen, at this stove, in this family, or at this desk,
in this schoolroom, on this tractor or assembly line, this
perhaps (to us) very unsatisfactory arrangement of things.

The wife of a long-distance truck driver wrote that she was
so thankful for what she called an "unusual, wonderful marriage." Her husband has had this job for two and a half years,
but each time he comes home "it's like a new romance. I
empathize with the single mothers, going to functions alone,

making decisions, changing the car tire, going to bed alone. The loneliness is hard, but my heart would break over the bitterness of divorce and the permanence of death.

"I rode with him for two weeks this summer and there is nothing romantic about long-haul trucking. How lonely to sit in a restaurant alone, or have a weekend layover and not be able to attend church. He spends time every day soaking up the Word (something it is hard to find time for at home).... Maybe I'm wrong. It seems that God has given us special grace, and I cannot see that these areas [learning to take hands off and trusting God] could have been exercised and strengthened in any other way."

I don't think she is wrong. The happiness they have found is *because* of the strain put on it by the man's job, or rather, I should say because of their *response* to the strain.

But will this work for me? someone may ask. Abandonment to the Lord always *works*—not in the same way for everyone, of course. He deals with us according to His intimate knowledge of who we are and what we need to bring us into conformity with the image of His Son. It is conformity to that image that God is working on all the time, and what an encouragement to me it is to know that He is not going to give up on me until it is accomplished! *We shall be like Him.* That is His promise.

A spiritual outlook brings peace. "Those who live on the level of our lower nature have their outlook formed by it, and that spells death; but those who live on the level of the spirit have the spiritual outlook, and that is life and peace.... You are on the spiritual level, if only God's Spirit dwells within you; and if a man does not possess the Spirit of Christ, he is no Christian" (Rom 8:5-6, 9).

When I think of the lovely picture Lilias Trotter gives us of the wild rose calyx, joyously flung back as the new dying brings a richer living, I think of two women I know who illustrate that. One of them, very much a woman of her generation, could not imagine giving up her job, her prestige, and her freedom in order to be a mother. That was too high a price to pay. But as she grew in grace she saw that giving herself to God meant giving Him everything—death to herself. Then He showed her that motherhood was His call, and when she obeyed she found not only peace but joys she had not dreamed of. Her yielding (a "death") meant that a richer life had begun to work in her heart, and wistful thoughts of all she had left behind (the "petals" that the calyx has let go) were forgotten in her happy embracing of that life.

St. Paul told the Philippian Christians that they were his pride and joy, proof that he had not run his race in vain. "But if my lifeblood is to crown that sacrifice which is the offering up of your faith, I am glad of it, and I share my gladness with you all. Rejoice, you no less than I, and let us share our joy" (Phil 2:17-18).

The other woman has been devastated not once but several times by Christian men who gave every indication of loving her and intending to marry her, and then have "ridden off into the sunset" with somebody else. She has chosen to surrender all her wounds to her Lord, believing against all odds that His purpose is love. She has made Amy Carmichael's prayer her own:

Lord, more and more
I pray Thee, or by wind or fire,
Make pure my inmost heart's desire
And purge the clinging chaff from off the floor.

I wish Thy way.
But when in me myself would rise
And long for something otherwise,
Then, Holy One, take sword and spear and slay.

Oh, stay near by,
Most patient Love, till, by Thy grace,
In this poor silver, Thy bright face
Shows forth in clearness and serenity.

What will it be
When, like the lily or the rose,
That in my flowery garden
I shall be flawless, perfect, Lord, to Thee?

(Rose from Brier. London: SPCK, 1950, p. 180)

🌿

THIRTEEN

Death in Us, Life in You

he maturing dandelion has long ago surrendered its golden petals, and has reached its crowning stage of dying. It stands ready, holding up its little life, not knowing when or where or how the wind that bloweth where it listeth may waft it away. It holds itself no longer for its own keeping, only as something to be shared. The delicate seed-globe must break up now; it gives and gives until it has nothing left.

THINK OF THOSE WHOSE LIVES have had the most significant impact on yours. Are they not men and women who were continuously giving themselves, loving sacrificially, and thereby giving us life? The maturing process in the Christian, as in the dandelion, is for one purpose: the giving of life. It gives and gives until it has nothing left—for itself. But it has given life— to new dandelions. So we in whom Christ dwells are the bearers both of His death and of His life. We are transmitters of life to the world.

Jesus' purpose in coming to our world could not be accomplished without His laying down His own life. "I have come that men may have life, and may have it in all its fullness. I am the good shepherd; the good shepherd lays down his life for the sheep" (Jn 10:10-11).

Each time the mystery of suffering touches us personally and all the cosmic questions arise afresh in our minds we face the choice between faith (which accepts) and unbelief (which refuses to accept). There is only one faculty by which we may lay hold of this mystery. It is the faculty of faith, and "faith is the fulcrum of moral and spiritual balance."

I write as one who has desperately needed a *refuge*. The bottom has dropped out of my world, as it were, more than once. What, exactly, was going on? Where was I to turn? To God? Is He God or is He not? Does He love me or does He not? Am I adrift in chaos or is the word true that tells me I am an individual created, called, loved, and purposefully placed in a *cosmos*, an ordered universe, a universe designed, created, and completely under the control of a loving God and Father?

It helps me, at such a time of bewilderment and sorrow, to go to some of the simplest words, such as *I am the good shepherd.* My Lord chose that description of Himself, and He does not change. He was and is and always will be my shepherd. The word fits my need, for I am a sheep, helpless and bleating. He cannot forget one for whom He lays down His life. I bank everything on that.

"Shall there be a mutiny among the flocks and herds, because their lord or their shepherd chooses their pastures, and suffers them not to wander into deserts and unknown ways?" wrote

Jeremy Taylor. I choose to believe, to surrender, to trust, and to accept. That much I can do. God then does what I can't do—"When the enemy shall come in like a flood, the Spirit of the Lord shall lift up a standard against him" (Is 59:19).

After the death of my husband Jim, I returned to my jungle station. My Quichua friends were sympathetic, for they had loved Jim, too. There was plenty of work to do, and I soon established new routines and was thankful for all the pressing duties that filled my days. Bags of mail began to come in bringing comfort and the assurance of prayers of hundreds of people, most of whom I did not know. I wrote to reassure my family and friends—I was all right, my baby Valerie was well, God was faithful—they need not be in anguish over the thought that I was "all by myself down there in the jungle." But my mother-in-law wrote of her fears that I was perhaps repressing my grief and might eventually crack. This upset me, of course, and I wondered if she was right. She was a chiropractor and a keen observer of human nature, a wise woman from whom I wanted to learn. But was there really no such thing as the peace that passeth understanding? Was I only imagining I had been given it? Could God fulfill His Word or couldn't He? The enemy came in like a flood and I had a whole new set of worries.

Another letter had "happened" to come in the same mail with Mom Elliot's, however, and I went back to that one often, for it contained a great antidote, another poem by Amy Carmichael:

When stormy winds against us break
Stablish and reinforce our will;
O hear us for Thine own Name's sake,
Hold us in strength, and hold us still.

🌿

Still as the faithful mountains stand,
Through the long, silent years of stress;
So would we wait at Thy right hand
In quietness and steadfastness.

So far the words sounded too brave and strong for me, but the last stanza set my feet on the Rock:

But not of us this strength, O Lord,
And not of us this constancy.
Our trust is Thine eternal Word,
Thy presence our security.

I was not strong. I was not constant or confident. But I had another much more dependable source of security, one guaranteed forever.

In the introduction to my biography of Amy Carmichael, *A Chance to Die*, I have tried to express the inexpressible debt of gratitude I owe to her. Her words are never empty to me. They are spirit and life. The ring of reality is there because she too knew what stormy winds could do to a soul, she knew long, silent years of stress, she knew her own weakness. She learned to accept suffering, even to accept it with joy, and, dying to her own natural reticence, "held herself no longer for her own keeping, but only as something to be shared." Her "deaths," of so many kinds, have resulted in *life*, for me and for many thousands.

"Continually, while still alive, we are being surrendered into the hands of death, for Jesus' sake," wrote Paul, "so that the life of Jesus also may be revealed in this mortal body of ours. Thus death is at work in us, and life in you" (2 Cor 4:11-12).

❧

Do the ways of God seem strange to some who are honestly seeking only to be good and faithful servants? There are stormy winds, long, silent years of stress, deaths to be died. The One we serve has not left us without inside information as to the why. All who would bring souls to God and multiply His kingdom must do so through surrender and sacrifice. This is what loving God means, a continual offering, a pure readiness to give oneself away, a happy obedience. There is no question of "But what about *me?*" for the motivation is love. All interests, all impulses, all energies are subjugated to that supreme passion.

Does it sound too high for us? But all of us know a little about it in so simple a thing as loving a child. Watch a grandfather in a restaurant with his small granddaughter. He has no thought whatever of himself. If she wants some of his french fries he would delight to give her all. He does not hold back, thinking, "But what about me?" He piles them onto her plate. What is the source of this delight and this self-obliteration? Very simple. The answer is love.

"To the soul that through 'deaths oft' has been brought to this point, even acts that look as if they *must* involve an effort, become something very natural, spontaneous, full of 'heavenly involuntariness,' so simply are they the outcome of the indwelling love of Christ" (Trotter: *Parables of the Cross*).

There are so many subtle forms of self to cling to—an insistence on my own judgment; confident in my own resources; an unconscious taking of my own way without even considering others; reluctance to hear a viewpoint opposed to my own; attempts to bring conversation around to my interests. If we ask the Lord to show us our selfishness He will do it—gently, one thing at a time, with help to face and renounce

FOURTEEN

The Last
Fragile Threads

ee in the wild iris pods how the last fragile threads must be broken, and with that loosing, all that they have is free for God's use in His world around. All reluctance, all calculating, all holding in is gone; the husks are open wide, the seeds can shed themselves unhindered.

BLAISE PASCAL, AUTHOR OF THE *Pensées*, was born in Clermont, France, in 1623. His mother died when he was three years old. Educated by his father, who was a government official, he was exceedingly precocious to the point of actually damaging his health by his intense application to studies. He became one of the greatest physicists and mathematicians of all time. When he was thirty-one he had a mystical experience while reading the seventeenth chapter of John, feeling the emptiness of his life suddenly filled with the presence of God. He called this his "second conversion," so crucial that he wrote notes about it which he sewed into the lining of his coat. It was found in the coat he was wearing when he died. The notes, in part, were these:

> Year of Grace 1654, Monday 23 November. . . . From about half past ten at night to about half an hour after midnight,

FIRE

> God of Abraham, God of Isaac, God of Jacob (Ex 3:6),
> not of philosophers and scholars.
> Certitude, heartfelt joy, peace.
> God of Jesus Christ.
> God of Jesus Christ.
> "My God and Your God" (Jn 20:17).
> "Your God shall be my God" (Ru 1:16).
> The world forgotten, everything except God. . . .
> Joy, joy, joy. Tears of joy.
> Jesus Christ.
> I am separated from him; for I have shunned
>   him, denied him, crucified him.
> May I never be separated from him.
> He can only be kept by the ways taught in the gospel.
> Complete and sweet renunciation.
> Total submission to Jesus Christ and to my director.
> Everlasting joy in return for one day's striving upon earth.
> I will not neglect your Word (Ps 119:16). Amen.

Pascal endured many kinds of suffering throughout his life, and during the last six months his physical suffering was intense. He prayed that he might endure it like a Christian. "Sick as I am, may I glorify You in my sufferings."

Here is one of the fifteen prayers he wrote asking God to use his sickness for His glory:

Take from me, O Lord, that self-pity which love of myself so readily produces, and from the frustration of not succeeding in the world as I would naturally desire, for these have no regard for your glory. Rather, create in me a sorrow that is conformable to your own. Let my pains rather express the happy condition of my conversion and salvation. Let me no longer wish for health or life, but to spend it and end it for you, with you, and in you. I pray neither for health nor sickness, life nor death. Rather I pray that you will dispose of my health, my sickness, my life, and my death, as for your glory, for my salvation, for the usefulness to your church and your saints, among whom I hope to be numbered. You alone know what is expedient for me. You are the Sovereign Master. Do whatever pleases you. Give me or take away from me. Conform my will to yours, and grant that with a humble and perfect submission, and in holy confidence, I may dispose myself utterly to you. May I receive the orders of your everlasting, provident care. May I equally adore whatever proceeds from you.

(*The Mind on Fire, An Anthology of the Writings of Blaise Pascal,* Multnomah Press, 1989, p. 291)

To Pascal, as to all in greater or lesser measure, it was *given* to suffer—"Unto you it is given in the behalf of Christ, not only to believe on him, but also to suffer for his sake" (Phil 1:29, AV). He relinquished his hold on his own life, his ambitions of accomplishment. All reluctance, all calculating, all holding in was gone.

"Unto you it is given ... to believe ... also to suffer."

The apostle who wrote those words was chained in prison because of his bold proclamation of the gospel. He was writing to believers who were suffering opposition as they contended for their faith, although they were not in prison. Suffering, he tells them, is a privilege.

Is it legitimate to apply his words to other kinds of suffering, such as Pascal's illness? We may well wonder how our particular kind of trouble (especially the trivial ones) can in any sense be said to be for Christ's sake. We are not in prison for speaking the truth. We are not being persecuted for our faith. Many in the world today endure great suffering that we in North America have never known. We have not been vouchsafed that privilege. Yet it seems to me that having something we don't want or wanting something we don't have, no matter how insignificant, is like learning the scales on the piano. They're a far cry from a fugue, but you can't play the fugue if you haven't mastered the scales. Our Heavenly Father sets the lessons suited to our progress. *All* are of His grace.

> He whose heart is kind beyond all measure
> Gives unto each day what He deems best—
> Lovingly its part of pain or pleasure,
> Mingling toil with peace and rest.
>
> (Lina Sandell *Norman Clayton's Favorites No. 2,*
> Norman Clayton Publishing Co., Winona Lake, Indiana, 1959)

Paul tells the young Timothy to be ready to take his share of suffering (2 Tm 1:8). I believe it is something given to us to be given back to Him. It *behooved* Him to suffer. Shall it not also, in some form, behoove us, His servants? We are not greater than He, and He knows our frame, knows best what kind to give. The writer to the Hebrews refers to the "race we have to run" implying that each has his own race, some one, some another, but all must run with faces toward Jesus Himself who gives the strength needed.

A friend wrote to tell me how she had been helped in the matter of irrational jealousy. Irrational though she knew it to be, her suffering was nevertheless very real and incapacitating. She simply could not bear to see her husband across a room talking with another woman. She knew very well that there was nothing inordinate in his relationship with this woman or any other woman, and recognized the problem as her own and her reaction as neurotic. Nevertheless it was there, it caused real pain, and she did not know what to do about it. One night after an evening in which she had seen him in conversation with several women, she and her husband had gone to bed, he to sleep and she to lie awake tormented by this demon of jealousy. She got up and went to another room where she knelt, and, placing in her hands, as it were, the emotion that seemed to be conquering her, she lifted her hands to the Lord, prayed aloud, and offered the whole matter to Him. Like the wild iris pod, she let go of the last fragile threads. Her testimony was that He simply *took* the offering, then and there, and in its place gave her peace. The plain physical act of turning the thing over to Him and receiving His peace in exchange helped to make it definite and final. She would not take it back, even if Satan tempted her later to think that she had not "really" committed it. She went back to bed relieved of her burden, and went peacefully to sleep.

Because we have such a staggering volume of information nowadays about other people's "problems," due to the inescapable bombardment of the mass media which includes daily screenings of emotional strip-tease on the talk shows, it is easy to assume that the gospel can't possibly be relevant to all of them. After all, it was written too long ago. Life has become overwhelmingly complex. Problems have arisen in our time that our grandparents never heard of. Everybody needs a specialized support group now, with an expert who is trained in "handling" their particular need. No doubt support groups can be helpful. Experts know things the rest of us are ignorant of. People are always asking me (I'm no psychologist and have never claimed to be one) to answer questions about their peculiar situations. Each time I think I've heard the worst, the next story tops it. I have no authority except the Word of God, but as I pray for help and search it for answers, I often find truth that applies. There is nothing new under the sun, as The Preacher said thousands of years ago, and "whatever is has been already, and whatever is to come has been already, and God summons each event back in its turn" (Eccl 3:15). The gospel is still the power of God for *salvation*—for all of us and for all of our needs.

Pascal's description of man in the seventeenth century perfectly describes man at the end of the twentieth: "dependency, desire of independence, need." His prayer gets at the heart of the solution: "You are the Sovereign Master. Do whatever pleases you. Give me or take away from me." Acceptance and relinquishment are the keys to our peace.

"May God show us every withholding thread of self that needs breaking still" (Trotter: *Parables of the Cross*).

FIFTEEN

Beaten Low
by the Storms

he seed-vessel hopes for nothing again. It seeks only the opportunity of shedding itself; its purpose is fulfilled when the wind shakes forth the last seed, and the flower-stalk is beaten low by the autumn storms. It not only spends but is "spent out" at last.

AS THE FIRST MISSIONARY IN ALGIERS, Lilias Trotter was often staggered by the immensity of the task of carrying the gospel across those desert wastes to the countless little villages hidden among the sandhills. After seven years she went to England, so exhausted she felt that she needed "weeks for prayer, but at present I don't seem to have sense for concentration in prayer or anything else, and am just vegetating, and writing up this journal, and drawing the pictures from very promiscuous notes in tiny notebooks, written and drawn on camel-back, or in stray moments while supper was cooking, or the beasts were lading."

The doctor said her nerves and heart were worn by the strain of the battle and by the climate. During one sirocco (a hot, oppressive, dust-laden wind from the Libyan desert) she recorded a temperature in the shade of one hundred sixteen degrees Fahrenheit. Added to these physical buffetings was the sense of evil and spiritual oppression. Many who have challenged the forces of darkness in places where gospel light has not shone for centuries testify to the reality of the opposition and the nearly tangible power it can have over them.

At a place called Morley Hall in England she wrote of "a lovely sense of what it meant to be 'buried with Christ'—not only 'dead' but 'buried,' put to silence in the grave; the 'I can't' and the 'I can,' put to silence side by side in the stillness of 'a grave beside Him' with God's seal on the stone, and His watch set that nothing but the risen life of Jesus may come forth." It being autumn she watched the acorns falling on the road outside her lodging and thought how they would never come to anything because they were only lying *on* the ground, not *in* it. She made a fresh commitment to *die* with Christ, to be a corn of wheat that falls *into* the ground.

Blow after blow fell when she returned to her mission work. Two girl-brides, fifteen and seventeen, who had become Christians, died by a slow-working poison undoubtedly administered by enemies of the gospel. A girl convert who had been faithful for years fell under the power of a sorceress and suddenly would have nothing to do with the missionaries. Evil drugs were used to turn the minds of other converts against them. Although there seemed nothing encouraging on the human side of things, Miss Trotter turned as always to the parables of the earth around her.

"In the face of the bleak sky and cold wind, four little

snowdrop buds have sat for the last two or three days with their chins on the earth, and now, today, one of them has reared itself up, pure and fearless on its stalk, with all the promise of spring."

She knew the power of prayer that passes all bounds of physical possibility. Thinking of the "dear mud houses of Tolga, the domed roofs of the Souf, and the horseshoe arches of Tozeur, and the tiled huts buried in prickly pear hedges in the hills," and her powerlessness to go to them (she and her colleagues had been forbidden to go to the South lands), she found an intensity of joy in praying for them, believing that she could through this medium more effectively "bring down the working of the Holy Ghost" than if she were allowed to go there in person. "One can shut the door, as it were, and stand alone with God, as one cannot on the spot with the thronging outward distractions of the visible." She was strengthened by the thought of Moses' unanswered prayer to enter the promised land. Centuries later he was allowed to stand on the mountain there with Jesus Himself. And Elijah, because he was denied his request to die, experienced the glory of the fiery chariot when it was God's time for him to go.

Like the flower-stalk, she was "beaten low" by many storms, She hoped for nothing for herself but "to spend and be spent," to measure her life by loss and not by gain, to be bread broken and wine poured forth.

Samuel Zwemer, another missionary to North Africa, wrote words which might describe Lilias Trotter's life there: "To be content to persevere in Gospel witness for more than a generation, when visible results are so small, is heroism of the highest order, a heroism not of this world" (*The Love that Was Stronger* by I.R. Govan Stewart).

The seed must break in order to let go the shoot, the leafbud must break to let go the leaf, the flowerbud break to let go the flower, the petals drop off to let the fruit form. So in the wondrous cyclical plan of the Creator, the purpose of each is fulfilled. The Son of man forsook the ivory palaces of heaven to fulfill His Father's plan: "You know how generous our Lord Jesus Christ has been: he was rich, yet for your sake he became poor, so that through his poverty you might become rich" (2 Cor 8:9).

He calls all of us to poverty—that total self-stripping which is detachment from all that this world has to offer. Some He calls to poverty in the narrower sense, doing without property or money. Money holds terrible power when it is loved. It can blind us, shackle us, fill us with anxiety and fear, torment our days and nights with misery, wear us out with chasing it. The Macedonian Christians, possessing little of it, accepted their lot with faith and trust. "Somehow, in most difficult circumstances, their overflowing joy and the fact of being down to their last penny themselves, produced a magnificent concern for other people" (2 Cor 8:2, JBP). They were living proof that it is not poverty or riches that determine generosity, and sometimes those who suffer the most financially are the ones most ready to share what they have. "They simply begged us to accept their gifts and so let them share the honour of supporting their brothers in Christ" (2 Cor 8:4, JBP).

We may be asked to accept poverty of another kind, something others are not aware of. Lilias Trotter had no impressive results to exhibit of her missionary labors as compared with thrilling tales coming from other lands in her time. She had accepted that poverty, "buried" with Christ, her grave sealed, as she said, that nothing but the risen life of the Lord Jesus should come forth.

A group of Sunday School leaders (of which my grandfather happened to be one, and my father, nine years old, was allowed to go along) visited her in 1907, asking to "see the work."

"Our first feeling was one of dismay," wrote Miss Trotter. "What *could* we show them in an hour? And again, what had we to show Americans with their big ideas and keen business minds—no hospitals, no schools, little organization, and no results to speak of for twenty years' fight in Algiers. Then came the clue in the old saying, 'Difficulty is the very atmosphere of miracle.' We brought the problem to God, and bit by bit, as we prayed, the outline of a programme evolved. We decided to show in all honesty, not what we *had* done, but what had *not* been done, and believe in God to use the very weakness of it all."

The day arrived, and the leader of the group reminded Miss Trotter that they had only an hour. They long outstayed the time as she showed them the maps she had arranged around her courtyard, "with their woefully thin firing line of stations, and the still sadder record given by tiny red flags of places visited once, and left again to their darkness; and photographs of the pathetic Christless faces of inland tribes and suchlike things."

And the outcome? Before the ship carrying the Americans reached Naples they had raised enough money to support six missionaries for three years. The Algiers Mission Band was constituted and a committee was formed in America.

God used "the very weakness of it all." The new commitment made at Morley Hall to be "buried with Christ" had prepared

Miss Trotter for the tragedies she had to face when she returned to her field, but that was not the end of God's story. Death was followed by resurrection, as for the flower stalk and the child of God it always is—in His time.

SIXTEEN

The Point of Despair

A bit of sphagnum moss shows the process [of death leading on to new life] in miniature. Stage after stage of dying has been gone through, and each has been all the while crowned with life. Each time that the crown has sunk down again into death, that death has once again been crowned in the act of dying. And the life all the time is the apparent thing; the daily dying that underlies it is hidden to the passing glance.

SPHAGNUM IS A LARGE GENUS OF MOSSES, certain species of which are highly absorptive and are used for surgical dressings. It grows only in swamps or water, and as each layer decays it is "crowned in the act of dying," that is, a new one comes to life on top of it. This is how certain kinds of peat are built up.

When at times sorrow is heaped upon sorrow we cannot help wondering if this time God *has* forgotten us. We think of His promise that He will never allow us to be tempted beyond our ability to bear, and it seems that He has forgotten that promise, forgotten to be gracious. If ever a man had reason to feel that it was Walter Ciszek, as he describes in *He Leadeth Me*. In a Soviet labor camp he was interrogated for weeks in an attempt to persuade him to cooperate, that is, actively to work with his captors in various schemes.

"Life in the camp was painted in its blackest and bitterest details, and it was pointed out to me how easily I could escape all that if I wanted to work for the NKVD. I was annoyed, and then ashamed again of my own indecisiveness. Why couldn't I just stand up and say no? Instead, I temporized. I took to playing a game of cat and mouse with the interrogator, asking for time to think over his various proposals."

Ciszek was given books on the history and philosophy of communism and quizzed on the contents. He was glad to prolong the arguments and thereby postpone the need for a final decision.

"Then one day the blackness closed in around me completely. Perhaps it was brought on by exhaustion, but I reached a point of despair. I was overwhelmed by the hopelessness of my situation. I knew that I was approaching the end of my ability to postpone a decision. I could see no way out of it. Yes, I despaired in the most literal sense of the word: I lost all sense of hope. I saw only my own weakness and helplessness to choose either position open to me, cooperation or execution. . . .

"I knew that I had gone beyond all bounds, had crossed over the brink into a fit of blackness I had never known before. It was very real and I began to tremble. . . . I had lost the last shreds of my faith in God. . . . Recognizing that, I turned immediately to prayer in fear and trembling. I knew I had to seek immediately the God I had forgotten."

God had not forgotten him. Suddenly he was consoled by the thought of the Lord in Gethsemane. He too had known fear and

❧

weakness as He faced suffering and death. His "not my will" was an act of total self-surrender, Ciszek was changed in that moment.

"I knew immediately what I must do, what I would do, and somehow I knew that I could do it. I knew that I must abandon myself entirely to the will of the Father and live from now on in this spirit of self-abandonment to God. And I did it. . . . God's will was not hidden somewhere 'out there' in the situations in which I found myself; the situations themselves *were* His will for me. What He wanted was for me to *accept* these situations from His hands, to let go of the reins and place myself entirely at His disposal. . . . It was the grace God had been offering me all my life, but which I had never really had the courage to accept in full" (Walter J. Ciszek, SJ: *He Leadeth Me*, Doubleday, New York, 1975, pp. 84-89).

Ciszek is one more witness in modern times to the astounding grace which has carried faithful believers through all dangers, toils, and snares.

"Flogged, imprisoned, mobbed; overworked, sleepless, starving. . . . Honour and dishonour, praise and blame, are alike our lot: we are the impostors who speak the truth, the unknown men whom all men know; dying we still live on; disciplined by suffering, we are not done to death; in our sorrows we have always cause for joy; poor ourselves, we bring wealth to many; penniless, we own the world" (2 Cor 6:5, 8-10).

The death of one layer of sphagnum prepares the matrix from which new life springs. The tiny dried fronds, so devoid of any vitality or usefulness in themselves, are vital and useful in the economy of the Designer. He takes their desolation and makes it life-giving. Without the dying, the sphagnum would not "still live on."

✺

I am thankful for the rare combination of an artist's eye and a clear spiritual eye given to Lilias Trotter. The picture of the sphagnum "crowned in the act of dying" lights up so beautifully for us the word of Hebrews 2:9, "In Jesus . . . we do see one who for a short while was made lower than the angels, crowned now with glory and honour because he suffered death, so that, by God's gracious will, in tasting death he should stand for us all." *Crowned because He suffered.* May we not unite ourselves with Him even in this? He died for us, as George MacDonald says, not that we might not suffer but that our sufferings might be like His. Think what this means. If we are His children, we share His treasures, and all that Christ claims as His will belong to us as well. "If we share in his sufferings we shall certainly share in his glory" (Rom 8:17, JBP).

There was a day in January of 1973 when I felt very close to desolation. My husband had his first radiation treatment for cancer, three and a half minutes under the eye of a machine the size of a freight car, making the noise of three motor boats. In the hallway was an ominous sign: DANGER—HIGH VOLTAGE. On the door of the waiting room, NUCLEAR MEDICINE. That morning I had sat thinking of what was to come, looking out on the bare dogwood twigs against a winter-blue sky, and on my little Scottish terrier, MacDuff, rejoicing and running in the snow as well as his short little legs would allow, snuffling and tossing his frosty black beard in ecstasy. In the waiting room that afternoon I watched the other patients go, one by one, into the chamber of horrors, until it was Add's turn. The few minutes he was gone were long to me, long enough to pray for him, and to think of all these things—the blue sky, the dogwood tree, my little MacDuff, the snow scene, the mysterious action of the betatron, and we ourselves, held in the Hand that made us all, the Hand that is laid on us with love and with loving words, FEAR NOT.

I was beginning very slowly to understand the reason suffering is referred to a number of times in the Bible as a gift, a concept which makes no more sense to the world's mind than the idea of Christ nailed to a cross—a stumbling block to Jews, folly to Greeks. But "divine folly is wiser than the wisdom of man, and divine weakness stronger than man's strength" (1 Cor 1:25). Things which are spiritually discerned cannot be discerned in any other way. The truths of the Kingdom of God cut straight across our natural mindset. But when there is nowhere to turn but to God, no explanations which satisfy either mind or heart except in His Word, it is then that the Spirit opens the understanding of those who turn to Him in their helplessness.

When I read my journal of 1973 I can discern the dawning of this radical reversal. I was thanking God for things I would never have learned to thank Him for without the suffering itself. And thanksgiving, in the midst of darkness, clears a way for grace. Walter Ciszek, dying the daily deaths of a labor camp, knew a horror of a darkness far greater than mine, but he gives me his word: God did not leave him alone. God was there, even when he had no consciousness of His presence. I can take his word for it that there are no depths to which I will be called to go where God will not be. Then I ask myself: but why do I need the word of anyone but God Himself? He has told me again and again and again that He is with me and will always be with me, in the deep river, the hot fire, the Valley of the Shadow. Yet I sometimes doubt Him. So, in His mercy, He brings along witness after witness, people who have learned dimensions of transforming grace impossible for them to have learned anywhere but where they were.

"Dying we still live on"; they say, "disciplined by suffering, we are not done to death; in our sorrows we have always cause for joy; poor ourselves, we bring wealth to many" (2 Cor 6:9-10).

Their look is very kindly when they add, "Where do *you* expect to find out what authentic faith is? Where will *you* prove the truth of the eternal Word?"

SEVENTEEN

The Deathblow

ithin a few hours (of fertilization) the throb of new life has spread right through the flower, with this first result, that the petals begin to wither. Fertilization marks the striking of the deathblow to all that went before.

IT IS NOT UNUSUAL FOR THOSE WHO take up the cross in the form of self-giving service and go out gladly for God, to suffer very soon some deathblow. Is it a sign that they have made a terrible mistake? Quite the opposite. It may be the harbinger of fruitbearing. The surrender of themselves and their rights, the joyful acceptance of the heavenly vision is like the flower's opening itself to receive the pollen. Lilias Trotter explains how, in the hour in which the stigma is able to grasp the pollen (blown by the wind, carried by bees or butterflies), a glutinous or velvety surface develops which grasps and holds the pollen grains. The grains in turn, with their sculptured points and ridges, lay hold at the same moment. The pollen sinks down into the innermost depths and starts a new creation. In a few hours there is the throb of new life, the protoplasm quickens the seed, and the first result is death: the petals begin to wither.

My dear friends Phil and Janet Linton (as a seminary student in 1978-79 Phil had been one of my lodgers. One day I found him and his roommate Kenny Dodd sitting on their beds wearing parkas and earmuffs, claiming that the room never got much above twenty below zero. We ran a Spartan household, I guess, but it wasn't *that* cold!)—in 1986 Phil and Janet were on their first furlough from North Africa where they are missionaries. On a Tuesday, three weeks before their second baby was due, Janet's doctor proclaimed all well. On Wednesday Janet became aware that the baby was not moving. That night she could not sleep. Phil prayed with her and tried to comfort her. Finally she slept a little, exhausted, but by 4:30 A.M. was awake again, holding very still, listening, waiting. She knew the baby was gone.

When the doctor's office opened the Lintons were there. He could find no heartbeat. Hospital tests confirmed that the baby was dead. A C-section was performed and the baby was placed in Phil's arms—a beautiful face, a perfect little girl with black hair.

"Through my grief as I watched him hold her tiny body and weep great sobs, his whole body shaking, I saw an incredible picture of a father's love, a father's heart. . . . The doctor found no explanation for her death. He assumes it was what they call a 'cord accident,' where somehow the baby crimped the cord and the blood supply was cut off.

Phil writes, "I remember standing next to Janet in the bonding room, holding Laura's body in my arms and I kissed her cheeks and talked to her, knowing she wasn't there, but asking the Holy Spirit to help me in my weakness.

🌿

"Later when I took Christopher (he was two) to visit, a sweet little gray-haired lady volunteer bent down and asked him, 'Do you have a new little brother or sister?' Christopher answered solemnly, 'We lost our baby,' and she glanced at me with a stricken expression. I picked up Christopher and almost ran to the elevator where mercifully the closing doors gave me a few minutes to stifle my sobs and regain my composure. . . . I am surprised to find myself now, three and a half years later, with tears welling up in my eyes as I remember that time. Although the wound was clean and uninfected, it was deep and maybe it will always be tender."

Janet's story goes on: "Phil and Christopher could be with me at any time, and even at two, Christopher knew our hearts were broken and grieved with us. God's people showed us much love, but every step was incredibly painful, such as leaving the hospital with other mothers who had babies in their arms, then going to a clothing store for a little gown and having to explain to the salesclerk that it didn't really matter much about style because our baby was to be buried in it.

"Even though they had given me a shot to dry up the milk, it came in anyway. I had nursed Christopher and knew the deep feelings of nurturing that nursing brings and longed for Laura so much. I knew the Lord Jesus was caring for her in heaven with perfect milk or whatever she needed, but I knew that I wanted to care for her too, desperately, with all my heart and my body.

"Where in all this pain was God's love? I couldn't feel it. I was almost numb with pain. I think I wrote to you that my emotions were like a ship being tossed in a raging storm at sea. I could not feel the truth of God's love for me at that time. What it felt like was that God had dealt me a cruel blow, as with a whip. But underneath all those raging emotions the truth lay. A lifetime of knowing Him had laid a strong foundation that quietly supported me.... I knew with my mind and heart what went deeper than my pain—that Jesus showed us once and for all what He is like and what kind of love He has for us, by dying on the Cross. And that is fact. History. Nothing, no circumstance, no matter how hard or painful can change that. He has showed us His character once and for all. Our circumstances are not the window through which we understand His love, but rather we must view our circumstances through His love.

"A second avenue of truth to my mind and heart was the blessing of having an earthly father who loves me, and who I know would never deal me a seemingly cruel blow without reason."

I wanted to write to Phil and Janet, but the loss of a child is a sorrow God has not asked me to face. I turned to Samuel Rutherford, the seventeenth-century Scottish minister, who did face it:

> Grace rooteth not out the affections of a mother, but putteth them on His wheel who maketh all things new, that they may be refined; therefore sorrow for a dead child is allowed to you, though by measure and ounceweights; the redeemed of the Lord have not a dominion or lordship over their sorrow and other affections, to lavish out Christ's goods at their pleasure.... He commandeth you to weep and that princely One took up to heaven with Him a man's heart to be a compassionate High Priest. The cup ye drink was at the lip of sweet Jesus, and He drank of it.... Ye are not to think it a bad bargain for your beloved daughter that she died—she hath gold for copper and brass, eternity for time. All the knot

✻

must be that she died too soon, too young, in the morning of her life; but sovereignty must silence your thoughts. I was in your condition: I had but two children, and both are dead since I came hither. The supreme and absolute Former of all things giveth not an account of any of His matters. The good Husband man may pluck His roses and gather His lilies at midsummer, and, for ought I dare say, in the beginning of the first summer month; and he may transplant young trees out of the lower ground to the higher, where they may have more of the sun and a more free air, at any season of the year. The goods are His own. The creator of time and winds did a merciful injury (if I may borrow the word) to nature in landing the passenger so early *(Letters of Samuel Rutherford)*.

The deepest lessons come out of the deepest waters and the hottest fires. One of God's greatest gifts, parenthood, always includes the gift of suffering, that we may be humbled and our faith refined as gold in the fire. Again we are not given explanations but, to hearts open to receive it, a more precious revelation of the heart of our loving Lord.

"For the Lord will not cast off forever: but though he cause grief, yet will he have compassion according to the multitude of his mercies. For he doth not afflict willingly nor grieve the children of men" (Lam 3:31-33, AV).

Affliction is the opener of the understanding. The psalmist wrote, "It is good for me that I have been afflicted; that I might learn thy statutes. . . . I know, O Lord, that thy judgments are right, and that thou in faithfulness hast afflicted me" (Ps 119:71, 75, AV).

Occasions of desperation prepare the way for the recognition of Christ Himself, as, for example, when

— the wine ran out at a party,
— a man lay helpless for thirty-eight years,
— a violent maniac could not be restrained,
— the disciples fished all night and caught nothing,
— a baby was born blind,
— huge crowds had nothing to eat,
— a great storm came up, putting the disciples in peril,
— two sisters were left desolate when their brother died,
— a child died, a widow's only son died.

Into each situation came Jesus, bringing His love, His healing, His peace. He still comes to those who ask Him. He is still *El Shaddai*, the God who is enough.

And so Janet and Phil have proved Him to be. Janet's letter continues:

"How have we grown since God allowed Laura's death? We certainly have experienced the principle of 2 Corinthians 1:3, 4—being able to comfort others with His comfort. Also Romans 8:38—nothing can separate us from His love. And there is more—somehow I felt like I was able to 'grow up' in Him a little more, to know that He is so much greater than I thought He was, that His truth stands any test, and that, as Lewis says, He is not a tame lion. I learned to trust and fear and love Him better. We also have a 'treasure' in Heaven. And the Lord has given us two sweet daughters since then."

The place where we must meet Him today is the cross where the Lord of the Universe dealt finally with death. It is no vague and silly optimism we speak of, no false mysticism, but a bowing in humble repentance and faith at the foot of that cross. We must be crucified with Christ. That is the beginning of the new life—the deathknell and the birthpeal ringing at the same time.

The resurrection happened. We believe it. We bank all our hopes on it. Jesus is alive. And yet ... and yet we sorrow. There is no incongruity between the human tears and the pure joy of the presence of Christ—He wept human tears too. Nor is there sin in grieving, provided we do not give way to it and begin to pity ourselves. It is still appointed unto man once to die, and those who are left must grieve, yet not as those without hope. Resurrection is a fact. There would be no Easter and no basis for Christian faith without it. Hence there is no situation so hopeless, no horizon so black, that God cannot there "find His glory."

> Crown Him the Son of God
> Before the worlds began,
> And ye who tread where He hath trod,
> Crown Him the Son of man;
> who every grief hath known
> that wrings the human breast,
> And takes and bears them for His own,
> that all in Him may rest   (Matthew Bridges).

EIGHTEEN

Perfectly Adapted

here is nothing arbitrary in the different shapes of the seed-vessels. . . . The fine sand-like grain of this snapdragon needs storing in a capsule—such a quaint one it is (whether most like a bird or a mouse sitting on a twig is hard to say)—but it is a perfectly adapted treasure-bag for the delicate things.

MY FRIEND JUDY SQUIER of Portola Valley, California, is one of the most cheerful and radiant women I know. I met her first in a prayer meeting at the beginning of a conference. She was sitting in a wheelchair and I noticed something funny about her legs. Later that day I saw her with no legs at all. In the evening she was walking around with a cane. Of course I had to ask her some questions. She was gracious, humorous, and forthright in her answer. Born with no legs, she has prostheses which she uses sometimes but they are tiresome, she said (laughing), and she often leaves them behind.

When I heard of a little boy named Brandon Scott, born without arms or legs, I asked Judy if she would write to his parents. She did. She told them that this was at least a hundred times harder for them than it would be for Brandon, for "a birth defect by God's grace does not rob childhood of its wonder, nor is a child burdened by high expectations."

Judy described her life not as less-than-average, or even average or ordinary, but as extraordinary, because she is convinced that a loving Heavenly Father oversees the creative miracles in the inner sanctum of each mother's womb (Ps 139), and that in His sovereignty there are no accidents.

We may look at the various ways in which each of us is called to suffer as the Master Designer's shaping of the vessels meant to bear the seed of the divine life. The design of each is directly related to the function, and thus He gives to each something unique to offer, something no other is capable of rendering back to Him.

The One who formed the perfect seed-vessels according to the shape of the seed they carry formed Judy, and Judy has a special message to bear, a testimony which deals a heavy blow to the "quality of life" arguments for abortion. She goes on:

"What we judge to be 'tragic—the most dreaded thing that could happen,' I expect we'll one day see as the awesome reason for the beauty and uniqueness of our life and our family. I expect that's why James 1:2 is a favorite verse of mine. Phillips' translation put it this way: 'When all kinds of trials and temptations crowd into your lives, my brothers, don't resent them as intruders, but welcome them as friends! Realize that they come to test your faith and to produce in you the quality of endurance.'"

Judy is the mother of three beautiful little girls who she said were "popping in and out" so that she couldn't think too deeply as she was writing her letter, "but I give you a moment of down-to-earth real life which I am good at, since I am a very 'earthy' person.

"Being Christian didn't shield my family from the pain and tears that came with my birth defect. In fact, ten years ago when David and I interviewed our parents for a Keepsake Tape, I was stunned to hear my mother's true feelings. I asked her to tell the hardest thing in her life. Her response: 'The day Judy Ann was born and it still is. . . . And yet when we as a family look back over the years, our reflections are invariably silenced by the *wonder* of God's handiwork.

"Getting married and becoming a mother were dreams I never dared to dream, but God, the doer of *all* miracles, intended that my life be blessed with an incredible husband and three daughters."

In closing, she tells the Scott family that they have been "chosen in a special way to display His unique Masterwork. I pray that your roots will grow deep down into the faithfulness of God's loving plan, that you will exchange your inadequacy for the adequacy of Jesus' resurrection power, and that you will be awed as you witness the fruits of the Spirit manifested in your family. 'What the caterpillar calls the end of the world, the Creator calls a butterfly.'"

So God fits us with exquisite precision, each according to his vocation, for the place He wants us to occupy. The apostle Paul uses the metaphor of a building, "the cornerstone being Christ Jesus himself. In him each separate piece of building, properly fitting into its neighbour, grows together in a temple consecrated to the Lord. You are all part of this building in which God himself lives by his spirit" (Eph 2:20-22, JBP).

Might Judy Squier have fit more properly into her place if she had had legs (and two hands—one of hers is deformed) like the

❧

rest of us? Would she have brought forth the particular fruits of holiness the divine wisdom had ordained? Her life, shaped as it is by what we would call radical limitation, is being shaped, *as it could not be without that limitation,* into the likeness of her Lord, so that she may shine with the special manifestation no other can claim. Power comes to its full strength in weakness, the Bible says, and Judy makes that truth visible. She lives her life in and through Him who, out of His own humiliation and poverty, manifested His messianic greatness. He emptied Himself, and was therefore highly exalted.

There is room here, of course, for serious misunderstanding. The lack of legs will not make a saint out of anybody. Externals do not create holiness. Unlike the little seed-vessels, we humans are empowered to respond to the will of God—negatively or positively. The body I live in, the genomes tucked into the nucleus of its hundred trillion cells, the year and place of my birth, are factors with which I had nothing to do. My acceptance of God-given conditions of life is a choice which is mine to make. Will I trust Him here? Will I obey? Will I be thankful, making praise "the permanent pulsation" of my soul?

"I could never be thankful if I was born with no legs," we might say. Was Judy born with some special talent for thanksgiving? I think not. Like the psalmist who said he would bless the Lord at *all* times, His praise would continually be in his mouth, I think she and Joni Eareckson Tada and my father (who lost an eye) and many others I know who live victoriously with many kinds of handicaps simply respond in faith to God, and receive, for the terrible odds against which they struggle, the all-sufficient grace He proffers. By grace they *welcome* the trial as a friend, as Judy's favorite verse puts it.

While no external circumstance can make a saint out of any

of us, neither can it hinder the making of a saint, as St. Francis de Sales points out:

> There is a different practice of devotion for the gentleman and the mechanic; for the prince and the servant; for the wife, the maiden, and the widow; and still further, the practice of devotion must be adapted to the capabilities, the engagements, and the duties of each individual. It would not do were the bishop to adopt a Carthusian solitude, or if the father of a family refused like the Capuchins to save money. . . . Such devotion would be inconsistent and ridiculous. . . .
>
> It is not merely an error but a heresy to suppose that a devout life is necessarily banished from the soldier's camp, the merchant's shop, the prince's court, or the domestic hearth. . . .
>
> Lot remained chaste whilst in Sodom, and fell into sin after he had forsaken it. Wheresoever we may be, we may and should aim at a life of perfect devotion.
>
> *(Introduction to the Devout Life)*

There is nothing arbitrary in the shapes of the seed-vessels. There is nothing arbitrary in the shape of our life's conditions. They are "perfectly adapted treasure-bags."

❦

NINETEEN

Yes to the New Life

lance back at the vetch seed-vessels. Why is it that the leaves which used to stand firm and fresh like those of the flowering clover, have begun to shrivel and turn yellow? It is because they have acquiesced wholly now in the death sentence of their new birth, and they are letting the new life live at the expense of the old.

IN THE MAIL THAT CAME TO MY JUNGLE station after Jim's death were many letters quoting Scripture. I was grateful for every one, but the verse which was more like "water from the well of Bethlehem" than all the others was this:

"These little troubles (which are really so transitory) are winning for us a permanent, glorious and solid reward out of all proportion to our pain. For we are looking all the time not at the visible things but at the invisible. The visible things are transitory: it is the invisible things that are really permanent" (2 Cor 4:17-18, JBP).

Those words clarified for me the alternatives. Little troubles versus big ones. Was widowhood a big one? It was indeed, if this world is the only plane on which it can be judged. I think I read that it's number one on the list of causes of stress.

Visible versus invisible. If I concentrated on my losses and all the very present evidences of Jim's absence, that permanent, glorious, and solid reward would be completely out of focus. I must start concentrating on the invisible for a change. That was where my treasure was now, for my heart was there in a way it never had been before.

And what of the transitory versus the intransitory? "All that grieves is but for a moment." It seemed a long "moment," but I knew that someday it would be seen as of no account. There was eternity to consider. Here was a new chance to *choose* happiness and peace. They were not something that merely "happened" to me because I was lucky or because my temperament was sanguine (it's melancholic). They were *given* in proportion as I chose to view my sorrow in the light of the intransitory and invisible.

The leaves of the vetch shrivel because they have acquiesced wholly now in the death sentence of their new birth. Everything that went before has to go. Everything is going to be new.

"We, who have died to sin—how could we live in sin a moment longer? Have you forgotten that all of us who were baptized into Jesus Christ were, by that very action, sharing in his death? We were dead and buried with him in baptism, so that just as he was raised from the dead by that splendid revelation of the Father's power so we too might rise to life on a new plane altogether. If we have, as it were, shared his death, we shall also share in his resurrection" (Rom 6:3-5, JBP).

Rise to live on a new plane? Live our new lives with Him?

❧

"But we have to live in the *real* world! We need something practical!"

Nothing is more real and practical than the Word of God. This world is not more real than the other world. It won't last nearly as long. The objection implies that God who made both worlds forgets that we're stuck in the here and now. He never forgets. He knows our downsitting and our uprising. He understands our thoughts before we think them. He traces all our paths, keeps close guard before and behind us, spreads His hand over us, knows us through and through. There is not a word on our tongues with which He is not thoroughly familiar. He forgets nothing (except our confessed sins). It is because He is so well acquainted with what it means to live in the here and now, understands so thoroughly the hidden places of our hearts and walked this lonesome valley Himself, that He shows us the pathway *through* our suffering, the only pathway that leads to glory. He is *touched* with the feeling of our weaknesses and therefore knows how to comfort us. The new plane, the new life is designed to be lived here and now.

How much depends on our choices, how much on the work of the Spirit of God? Don't ask. Both truths are clear but hard to harmonize intellectually. I only know that the more I take at face value what He says and choose to open myself to His grace, the more I discover the eminent practicality of His Word. He makes available to us the very same power that raised our Lord Jesus from the dead. If we want His peace and obey Him, even in the least measure, He gives it.

"If by the Spirit you put to death all the base pursuits of the body, then you will live" (Rom 8:13). There it is in one verse: by the *Spirit you*—the work of the Holy Spirit and my will, in combination. Grace working on nature.

Libraries of books have been written about this new resurrection life, but this book happens to be about suffering. How shall we rise to this "new plane altogether" if we are newly widowed, sick, paralyzed, abused, abandoned? What difference does it make *here* that we were "dead and buried with him in baptism"? That was the dividing line between the old life and the new. That was the beginning of our life in Christ. The difference, a very great one, is figured in the vetch leaves—a complete acquiescence in the death sentence of the new birth.

I had no idea of all that when, at the age of ten, I wanted to be born again. It was very simple. I took God at His word, "received" Him, and was given the power to become a child of His. I sang songs like

At the Cross, at the Cross,
   Where I first saw the light,
And the burden of my heart rolled away,
   It was there by faith I received my sight,
And now I am happy all the day.

I cannot claim that overnight I became "happy all the day," but the Spirit of God began to show me that my once-in-a-lifetime choice must be followed by moment-by-moment choices to do things His way or mine. I must accept not just "salvation," meaning a free ticket to heaven, but His sovereign lordship of my life, His will (which often cut across mine). More than half a century later I am still learning the acquiescence of the vetch leaves, submission to the death-life cycle. I have not found the lesson "a piece of cake." In some ways it gets harder—

But we never can prove the delights of His love
    Until all on the altar we lay,
For the favor He shows and the joy He bestows
    Are for them who will trust and obey.   (J.H. Sammis)

October 25, 1972, was rather a full day in Hamilton, Massachusetts. I wrote in my journal of having finally found an apartment for my aging mother; of visiting a friend whose only son had been killed; of talking with Jill whose three-year-old son had a serious heart condition, and of taking my husband to the hospital because of a lip sore that did not heal. I wrote on a scrap of paper (perhaps in the hospital waiting room):

How to deal with suffering of any kind:
1. recognize it
2. accept it
3. offer it to God as a sacrifice
4. offer yourself with it

The diagnosis was cancer, and a date was set for surgery. Next night at home rectal bleeding occurred. My journal: "fear, resentment, worry—all very real for both of us, all necessitating coming to Christ." Here was my chance to "acquiesce wholly now in the death sentence" of the new birth, accepting to the uttermost limits the meaning of the cross.

The reason for the fear, resentment, and worry presented me once more with a dilemma and a choice. It was a *crux* (the Latin word for cross), crucial (a derivative of the same word) to my living in harmony with God—agreeing that it was not I, but Christ. Not my life, His. I am not my own, I am bought with a price; therefore I belong to Him and what happens to me is His affair. The old life, mine, is gone. Crucified. Dead. The new life—the daily *yes, Lord*—lives at the expense of the old. Both cannot flourish together. It's one or the other. It's no to the self, yes to the Lord.

P.T. Forsyth wrote, "Our will alone is our ownest own, the only dear thing we can and ought really to sacrifice" (*The Cruciality of the Cross*, Wm. Eerdmans Publishing Co., Grand Rapids, no date given, p. 92).

What if I have to go through deep waters? Will He be there? It is YES to the deep waters:

> Thou didst cast me into the depths, far out at sea,
>   and the flood closed round me;
> all thy waves, all thy billows, passed over me.
> I thought I was banished from thy sight
> and should never see thy holy temple again.
>   The water about me rose up to my neck;
>   the ocean was closing over me.
>   Weeds twined about my head
>   in the troughs of the mountains;
>   I was sinking into a world
>   whose bars would hold me fast forever.
> But thou didst bring me up alive from the pit,
>   O Lord my God   (Jon 2:3-6).

What of the furnace? "See how I tested you, not as silver is tested, but in the furnace of affliction; there I purified you. For my honour, for my own honour I did it" (Is 48:10-11). It means YES to the fire, the process essential to our purifying. We have said YES to the burning out of the impurities, which the apostle Peter tells us is nothing extraordinary—everybody ought to expect it, in other words. But the fire of suffering is still the fire of suffering. The apostles never for a moment denied the reality. They wrote about it often, pointing repeatedly to that other level on which it was to be seen: "I reckon that the sufferings we now endure bear no comparison with the splendour, as yet unrevealed, which is in store for us. . . . If we hope for something we do not yet see, then, in waiting for it, we show our endurance" (Rom 8:18, 25).

TWENTY

Suffering Love

*T*he great North African aloe plant is like our *annuals on a larger scale, for it flowers and seeds but once in its career, though that numbers more years than these can count weeks. Up till then its thick hard leaves look as if nothing could exhaust their vigor. The flower stalk pushes up from a fresh sheaf of them—up and up twelve or fourteen feet—and expands into a candelabra of golden blossom, and not a droop comes in the plant below.*

But as the seed forms, we see that death is forming apace, slowly but surely. The swords lose their stiffness and color . . . they have become but limp, grayish-brown streamers.

ONE WHO IS ABOUT TO BECOME A GRANDMOTHER wrote to me of her love-longing for the unborn child, but the love is pierced with pain, for the mother-to-be, her daughter-in-law, refuses to have anything to do with her. She is "about to die" over this. Will she not be allowed to see the child, to rejoice with her son and daughter-in-law? Will she be denied the bliss of holding the baby?

I know a grandmother who endured precisely that kind of pain for a long time, so I asked her if she would answer the letter. What she wrote applies so exactly to so many different kinds of suffering that I asked her permission to use the letter:

I will distill some of the principles that kept me from "going under." In no way think any of these were done easily or that I am taking a simplistic route. The road you are on is excruciatingly painful and in many ways will be a means of identifying with Christ in His sufferings of rejection. Colossians 1:24 ("It is now my happiness to suffer for you. This is my way of helping to complete, in my poor human flesh, the full tale of Christ's afflictions still to be endured, for the sake of his body which is the church.") is one of the most powerful statements on suffering in this regard, I think.

God is intensely interested in forming Christ in our character and we can assume that He is going to do this in you and your dear daughter-in-law. So:

1. THANK Him over and over and over again for what He is doing through this experience.

2. SING about His mercies and greatness. The enemy would like to destroy your family and your joy—all you have invested and all your hopes for the future. Second Chronicles 20:1-30 tells a wonderful story. Their families were about to be destroyed. Read it carefully and you will see how:

a. They were afraid (v. 3)

b. They sought the Lord (v. 3)

c. They did not need to fight. God said He would do it for them (v. 17)

d. They were not to fear or be dismayed (a choice, a decision) (v. 17)

e. Singers were appointed to go *ahead* of the warriors in the most vulnerable position (v. 21)

f. They were to sing of the *mercies* of God. Why mercies? Because they weren't any better than the enemy and they were saying, "We don't deserve to live but we are children of the most High God. We are totally dependent on His mercies and love." (v. 21)

g. When they sang the Lord sent ambushments. Victory came (v. 22). Sing when you are vacuuming, cooking, walking, driving, trying to go to sleep, showering—decide to sing. Declare to those in the heavenlies that your God is able to deliver. Satan will fear. His minions will fear.

3. CONCENTRATE on *your reactions* to her and not on what she is doing. At the present you are in bondage to her. You can get free of this bondage. Perhaps you'll need to get free before she can get free herself. *So,* when she does something against you, or you feel her intense dislike, immediately your natural response is fear, hurt, dismay, sadness, anger, or wishing she were dead. Now then:

4. TAKE THAT RESPONSE and go to our Father and say,

a. Father, I confess my resentment (or whatever the response is regarding this situation) as sin (don't leave that out or substitute the word "tendency," or be tempted to call it anything other than sin. We do have an antidote for sin.)

b. I repent of my sin.

c. Please forgive me.

❧

d. Please forgive her.

e. I receive your forgiveness based on Your Word.

The first two are so terribly important. Say this out loud if possible, and say it as the memory of some incident comes to your mind. Then:

5. ACCEPT His forgiveness.

6. MAKE A LIST of the grievances and go through this simple prayer over each incident. Then:

7. TEAR UP the grievances.

God Himself will begin to act on your behalf and hers. She needs you and you need her. Blessings on you, dear one, and Bon Courage!

I love the emphasis on thanksgiving and singing right at the start, not easy things to do when, in the midst of pain, we are trying to grasp spiritual truth. But here is the lesson of the aloe—simple, visible, graspable. There will be no life-giving seed unless all is given over first to death. Before Jesus suffered death on the cross He suffered the death of being despised and rejected. Sooner or later human love has to suffer, and when there is rejection, even in less serious forms than those the grandmother described, we are initiated into the fellowship of suffering love. All must give way to that indwelling life, all the corruptible must be let go, as the aloe's swords are drained of vitality. The plant does not concentrate on the death process. It's far better to concentrate on our own reactions to the offender than on the list of offenses, and then to take those reactions to the Father. In this way we may be rid of the "carnal," letting it go to death, in order that, as we are growing in conformity to Christ's death, we are growing also in conformity to His life. He is increasing, and I am decreasing.

The tearing up of the list of grievances is a clear and deliberate renunciation, symbolizing our wholehearted severance from the wrong, and our determination to live for Him who died for us.

If my friend had not found in her quota of suffering God's liberating answer, and been obedient to it, she would not have been qualified to help the other grandmother. She was able to help complete, in her poor human flesh, Christ's sufferings, for the sake of His body, of which my correspondent is also a member. Life received is life that can be passed on. I don't suppose she was thinking of how she might later help others. She was probably very much occupied with the pain of rejection and the sorrow of not being able to get her hands on the precious child. But we are seldom shown in advance God's intention in a particular trial, nor the long-term effect our obedience may have on others.

The hard shell of our self-protection must give way. The thick, hard leaves of the aloe must become limp and helpless. Thus only is their life given to the formation of the seed. Thus our hearts must at times be wrung till we feel helpless, but God is not finished with us.

TWENTY-ONE

The Winds
of the Lord

*ne day's sirocco in May will turn a field, bright
with the last flowers, into a brown wilderness,
where the passing look sees nothing but ruin. Yet in that
one day the precious seed will have taken a stride in its
ripening that it would have needed a month of ordinary
weather to bring about; it will have drawn infinite life out
of the fiery breath that wrought havoc with the visible.*

THE ANSWER TO OUR WHY about suffering is, as we have noted,
not immediate or abstract. It is a call to come follow. As we
walk through our common duties in the company of Jesus we
learn what the taking up of the cross is all about. In what we
thought of as our strong points we find unsuspected weakness—a chance to die! In what we felt quite adequate to
perform we discover that we need help—perhaps from someone
we thought of as our inferior—another chance to die! It is an
unsettling business, this being made conformable to His death,

and it cannot be accomplished without knocking out the props. If we understand that God is at work even when He knocks out the small props, it will not be so difficult for us to take when He knocks out bigger ones.

The very week which I had looked forward to to begin the writing of this book found me dragging around with what appeared to be merely a heavier-than-usual cold, accompanied by a deep cough. I tried to work at my accustomed place and pace. Somehow I couldn't. I could not grasp a thought, hold onto it firmly, and carry it through to its logical conclusion. A day or two went by with little to show. I took myself by the scruff of the neck—"Get *on* with it!"—but found that a prop had been knocked out. I had a fever. Only a degree or two, but enough to scramble my brains, and a salutary reminder that normal health and the ability to do ordinary work are gifts from God for which I should thank Him every day of my life. A letter "happened" (was ordained) to come then, remarking that God is much more interested in making us holy than He is in getting a job done. My thought had been that whatever was wrong with me a nuisance. I was disturbed by my inability to get the job done. The letter made me pause. The interruption was more important (for the appointed duration) than the book. *Think*, God was saying to me, *what you are writing about*.

"...in that one day the precious seed will have taken a stride in its ripening that it would have needed a month of ordinary weather to bring about."

A visit to the doctor confirmed that what I had was not an ordinary cold and could have turned into something less than ordinary. I had not been sick for so many years I had forgotten what a degree of fever can do—the restlessness, the impossibility of finding a comfortable position, and the wild, incoherent dreams of half-sleep which awakened memories of my only experience of ether, fifty-five years ago. The brief siege effectively knocked out the props, yet its very brevity and triviality made me think of the really ill, and ask myself again whether, in even thinking of attempting a book on suffering, I was perhaps exercising myself in great matters, things too high for me. The answer, of course, was yes. I am always doing that. The subject is far beyond either my intelligence or my personal experience. But the things most worth writing about are all "too wonderful for me," things so high that I cannot attain unto them—nor, I suppose, can anyone who measures his own pain by the pain of the thorn-crowned and crucified King.

Yet I write, drawing on the witness of others who know so much more, with the hope that some who might not have found *their* writings will be glad to find a few of their treasures here.

Amy Carmichael knew much of pain, many kinds of pain—chronic severe headaches and neuralgia, broken bones, twisted back, cystitis, twenty years of confinement to her room. In her *Rose from Brier* she writes,

In Southern India the wind is often hot, and a hot air rises like a burning breath from the ground. . . . Such a wind parches the spirit, drains it of vitality, sends it to seek some cool place, caring only to find a shadow from the heat. But be the wind scorching, or sharp and cold, it can only cause the spices of His garden to flow out.

Her reference is to the *Song of Songs*, "Awake, O north wind; and come, thou south; blow upon my garden, that the spices thereof may flow out" (Sg 4:16, AV).

In Aleksandr Solzhenitsyn's *Cancer Ward,* Dontsova, the doctor who had dealt for thirty years with other people's illnesses, reading the X-rays and the imploring eyes of her patients, finds that she herself has a malignant tumor. Until that moment she saw all human bodies as identical, according to the standard text. She knew the physiology and pathology.

Then suddenly, within a few days, her own body had fallen out of this great, orderly system. It had struck the hard earth and was now like a helpless sack crammed with organs—organs which might at any moment be seized with pain and cry out....

Her world had capsized, the entire arrangement of her existence was disrupted. She was not yet dead, and yet she had had to give up her husband, her son, her daughter, her grandson, and her medical work as well, even though it was her own work, medicine, that would now be rolling over her and through her like a noisy train. In a single day she had to give up everything and suffer, a pale-green shadow, not knowing for a long time whether she was to die irrevocably or return to life.

It had once occurred to her that there was a lack of color, joy, festivity in her life—it was all work and worry, work and worry. But how wonderful the old life seemed now! Parting with it was so unthinkable it made her scream.

[Bantam Books, Grosset and Dunlap, New York 1969, pp. 445f]

I was reminded of St. Augustine's words, "The very pleasures of human life men acquire by difficulties." Sometimes we recognize them only in retrospect. On one of those terrible days during my husband's cancer, when he could hardly bear the pain or the thought of yet another treatment, and I could hardly bear to bear it with him, we remarked on how wonderful it would be to have just a single *ordinary* day. Some who read this may be in just that sort of place, the entire arrangement of existence disrupted. It makes you scream. God speaks to you: *It is I. Do not be afraid.*

Paul found Him in his hunger, shipwreck, floggings, imprisonment. "I have been very thoroughly initiated into the human lot with all its ups and downs" (Phil 4:12). The winds of God had blown upon him in many ways—handicapped, puzzled, persecuted, knocked down. Yet he was able to say that he was never frustrated or in despair, never had to stand it alone, was never knocked out. And here's why: "Every day we experience something of the death of Jesus, so that we may also show the power of the life of Jesus in these bodies of ours" (2 Cor 4:10, JBP).

The winds of God blow on all of us. When it is the hot sirocco everything in life turns into a brown wilderness, nothing but ruin. But that is only the visible. Remember that word about the outward man suffering wear and tear while the inward receives fresh strength (2 Cor 4:16)? Remember the little, transitory troubles (the thousand deaths), the mere visible things, and what they will win for us? Remember the psalm which says, "For Thy sake we are killed all the day long. . . . Wherefore hidest thou thy face and forgettest our affliction and our oppression? For our soul is bowed down to the dust" (Ps 44:22, 24-25, AV)? Remember the promise of the weight of glory, the permanent, glorious, solid reward out of all proportion to our pain?

Find a quiet place. Be quiet. Ask God to help you to look entirely away from the visible to the invisible. Look away from the transitory to the permanent. All influences, circumstances, and conditions (yes, all of them) are designed with the glory of infinite life in mind—in the Mind that knows it all from beginning to end.

Old age can seem like a hot wind, whistling in from some unseen desert, withering and dessicating with a speed that takes our breath away. Wear and tear make their indelible marks on the face in the mirror which (weirdly and shockingly sometimes) becomes the face of a stranger. Fear grips us as we take note of what has gone and contemplate what is to come. The spectres of loneliness, illness, abandonment, and the serial deprivation of our powers stare back at us from the furrowed and sagging face. But God will be there. There is no need to fear the future, *God is already there,* and God's promise for us is, "They shall still bring forth fruit in old age" (Ps 92:14, AV).

I have not quite reached the biblical norm for man's lifespan, so perhaps I have a few more years. I will not be growing younger, but I want to be growing holier. When Malcolm Muggeridge returned to his cottage in Sussex after his last trip overseas he said he was going home to get ready to die (or something to that effect). He is an old man, but hear the words of one Jim Elliot who died at twenty-eight: "When it comes time to die, make sure that all you have to do is die." The only way to make sure of that is to live every day as though it were your last.

I pray that I may be responding *now* to all the Lord's dealings, for I know that the best fruit will be what is produced by the best-pruned branch. The strongest steel will be that which went through the hottest fire and the coldest water. The deepest knowledge of God's presence will have been acquired in the deepest river or dungeon or lion's den. The greatest joy will have come forth out of the greatest sorrow.

> Let no one think that sudden in a minute
>   All is accomplished and the work is done.
> Though with thine earliest dawn thou
>   shouldst begin it,
> Scarce were it ended with the setting sun.

(F.W.H. Meyers: St. Paul)

TWENTY-TWO

The One Thing Necessary

*T*he plant has nothing to "mind" now but the treasure it bears. Its aim has become absolutely simple. In the old carnal days there was the complexity of trying to carry on two lives at once, nourishing root and stem, leaf and flower and tendril, alongside the seed-vessel and seed. All that is over. It withdraws itself quietly into the inner shrine where God is working out that which is eternal.

A DEAR FRIEND IN HUNGARY has chosen the simple way over the complex. She writes, "My longing for a husband is there, but I offered it up to the Lord. Often I imagine a single future for myself. In fact, the presence of a man in my life would be an unexpected gift. Thank you for praying for me. I wouldn't like to put my own imagined happiness before God's greater glory."

Another who is earnestly trying to learn that abandonment wrote, "I long for marriage and motherhood, but I also want to please God. Are these desires diametrically opposed?" I could not tell her that God would fulfill both, but I assured her there was nothing sinful in the desire for marriage and motherhood. It was perfectly human and normal, but like all our dreams of human happiness must be surrendered as the Hungarian girl's were, to the one supreme aim: the glory of God, which always leads in the end to more than happiness—to fullness of joy, pleasures forevermore. If she could best glorify God by being married, she could be sure He would, in His time, give her a husband.

The Virgin Mary was one whose aim was absolutely simple. She is an icon of radiant simplicity, single-eyed, with nothing to "mind" but to please her Master. When He sent His angel with an earth-shattering message, her answer was quick and unequivocal: yes.

Acceptance of the will of God is always a simple thing, though for us who are yet far from sainthood it is often not an *easy* thing. Our lives are still complicated, our aims mixed, our vision clouded. No wonder Jesus told us to consider the birds and the lilies. We spend much time in talk, we write books about deep things, but we miss seeing God's little chickadee as he flits cheerily in the snow-laden evergreen, finding the seed God has put there for him. We rarely consider a bird in his precious simplicity—the chickadee, wearing his little black cap and gray suit, whistling tinily, doing nothing but what he was made to do.

I would like to do nothing but what I was made to do. I am sure this is what God intends. How shall I know what that is except in quietness? How listen if I am full of talk? I must cease the rehearsal of personal wants and feelings, willingly release things that seem important but in fact have nothing to do with my true goal. The itch to know and to have and to be anything other than what God intends me to know, to have, and to be must go.

This is a far cry from quietism. It may sound to some like an indolent and sluggish way of life, mere spiritual torpor, perhaps even the Eastern ideal of absence of desire. "And yet I do speak words of wisdom to those who are ripe for it," wrote Paul, "not a wisdom belonging to this passing age, nor to any of its governing powers, which are declining to their end; I speak God's hidden wisdom, his secret purpose framed from the very beginning, *to bring us to our full glory*" (1 Cor 2:6-7, italics mine).

If we truly believe that God wants to bring us to our full glory, we will long increasingly to unite our wills with His. It is in exact proportion as we do this that we will find happiness here on earth. If His will is done on earth, it becomes like heaven, where His will is always done.

"Happiness, Heaven itself, is nothing else but a perfect conformity, a cheerful and eternal compliance of all the powers of the soul with the Will of God" (Samuel Shaw, 1669).

When something interrupts what we are doing (the angel interrupted Mary's housework, I suppose), we fret. As I write, two dear aged aunts, sisters, lie in the hospital. What will I do if one of them dies while I must be on a speaking trip? This is the sort of question that can quickly destroy my peace. God restores it when I review my goal: to please Him. Nothing except my own will can interrupt that. Nothing on earth. It is the only thing I must "mind," and I am assured that He will enable me to mind it, no matter what. If Aunt Anne or Aunt Alice should die when the funeral would conflict with my commitment to speak, God is not taken by surprise, I do not

🌿

doubt that He will make plain my duty when the time comes, and until then *it is not my concern*. We make our lives insupportably complex by disobeying Jesus' command to take no thought for tomorrow. Planning for tomorrow, when planning is necessary and possible, belongs properly to today. Worrying about tomorrow belongs nowhere. The Lord gives us daily, not weekly, bread. He gives strength according to our days, not our years. The work, the suffering, the joy are given according to His careful measure.

And if I, who am perfectly well, am tempted to worry about the mere interruption of a few days' schedule, what of the two aunts themselves and all others whose lives seem to have come to a screeching halt because of illness? Can *they* continue to fulfill the will of the Father, inert on a sickbed? Surely they can. "This illness will not end in death," Jesus said when told that Lazarus was sick. "It has come for the glory of God" (Jn 11:4). Sickness—for the glory of God? Jesus could not have raised Lazarus from his grave and thus shown God's glory if Lazarus had not been sick. The glory of God may be revealed through sick people in ways other than resurrection. Most of us have witnessed His glory in the forms of patience, serene trust, unselfishness, gratitude, and other divine graces in the ill, but even in the absence of such evidence we can trust Him to look after His own glory in His own way. The Father knows the frame and remembers that it is mere dust. His compassions never fail. His arms hold us when we are too weak to cling, His Spirit prays in us and for us in those groanings which never find words. His salvific work goes on when we feel like stragglers making not an inch of progress.

God's message to Mary would have seemed to most engaged girls an enormous inconvenience, even a disaster. It caused her a moment of puzzlement (how could this be?), that was all. She raised no objections, no questions about what would happen to her or her fiancé. Her answer, fruit of perfect trust, came very simply, "Be it unto me according to Thy word."

The word of the prophet Habakkuk may come to some of us when everything appears to have come to nothing, "Although the fig-tree does not burgeon, the vines bear no fruit, the olive-crop fails, the orchards yield no food, the fold is bereft of its flock and there are no cattle in the stalls, yet I will exult in the Lord and rejoice in the God of my deliverance" (Hb 3:17-18). It is amazing what praise can do when we're in the bottom of the barrel, so to speak!

"This one thing I do" was Paul's motto. He was always moving "with hands outstretched to whatever lies ahead" (Phil 3:14, JBP)—straight for the goal, to fulfill his calling. But what a great number of apparent setbacks he suffered! Prison, for example. When it was possible to avoid prison Paul avoided it. (Let no one take it that we are never to fight wrongs or disabilities or setbacks.) When there was no way to avoid it, he regarded it as no setback at all. He wrote to the Ephesians that they were not to lose heart because of this—in fact, they ought to feel honored, for to him had been entrusted the grace of carrying the gospel to the Gentiles. It would cost him something, but his being bound in prison chains did not in the least frustrate the purpose of God. We might say it was "par for the course," the course of obedience, all taken into account in advance in God's plans. As Corrie Ten Boom used to say, "God has no problems, only plans." Paul referred to "the complex wisdom of God's plan," which angelic powers needed to see being worked out through the church, "in conformity to that timeless purpose which he centred in Christ Jesus, our Lord"

(Eph 3:10-11, JBP). Consider those attentive angelic powers, spectators of *us* (for we Christians compose the church). Do we give thought to our vital part in the unfolding of the complex wisdom of God's timeless purpose? While angels wait and watch, our part is to be simple—simply to trust, simply to obey, and leave the complexities to the Engineer of the universe.

Nothing would upset our equilibrium if our goal were pure and simple, as was Paul's. When, as a prisoner, he was taken on a voyage across the Adriatic Sea, an angel stood beside him and told him not to be afraid, in spite of winds of hurricane force, for God would spare his life and the lives of all on board. Paul cheered his guards and fellow passengers with the good news, but the bad news was that they would have to run aground on some island (Acts 27:26).

It would seem that the God who promised to spare all hands might have "done the job right," saved the ship too, and spared them the ignominy of having to make it to land on the flotsam and jetsam that was left. The fact is He did not, nor does He always spare us. Running aground is not the end of the world— sometimes it fits in very neatly with God's running of the world. It certainly helps to make the world a bit less appealing to us, drawing our attention to a far better one. Even disaster cannot destroy the peace of one whose aim is absolutely simple.

It was not until years after my first bereavement that I heard about "grief work," and studies of what were called the five stages of grief. I do not know whether these are considered necessary for all, but I suppose if I had heard of them I might have felt obliged to move consciously through each at that time. Perhaps my memory of the early months of my widow-hood is selective, but I am sure that in spite of very real grief

God met me in ways psychology knows nothing about. He gave me peace which was quite beyond explanation, and at times an exuberance of joy that was, as Scripture confirms, "unspeakable." Thomas à Kempis knew the simpler way, "a pure and whole forsaking of ourselves and of our own will, that we might get freedom of spirit." One of his dialogues with God went like this:

> My son, if thou wholly resign thyself into my hands and take nothing to thee again, thou shalt have the more grace of me.
>
> O Lord, how oft shall I resign me to thee, and in what things shall I forsake myself?
>
> Always and in every hour, in great things and in small! I except nothing; for in all things I would find thee naked and poor, and void of thine own will. How mayst thou be mine and I thine, unless thou be clearly bereft of thy own will, within and without? And the sooner that thou canst bring it about, so much the sooner shall it be better with thee. . . . Resign thyself wholly to me and thou shalt have great inward peace" (Book III, Chapter 37).

The five stages of grief work may be unavoidable if we feel ourselves adrift in a universe without meaning, but may there not be some shortcuts to peace for those who truly believe in the Shepherd, and go gently with him through the Valley of the Shadow?

TWENTY-THREE

A Breaking-up and a Breaking-down

Contemplate the last stage in the plant, before the inwrought life is free for use. There is a breaking-up and a breaking-down such as it never had before. Such brittleness comes as the seed ripens that it is almost impossible to pick some of the stems without cracking them in two or three places. The ripening seed-vessels share the same brittleness; you can hardly touch them without the whole crown falling to pieces in your hand.

WHEN THE YOUNG AUGUSTINE HAD WANDERED far from God, his mother Monica wept for him "more than mothers weep for the bodily deaths of their children," he wrote. "For she, by that faith and spirit which she had from Thee, discerned the death wherein I lay, and Thou heardest her, O Lord; Thou heardest her, and despisedst not her tears, when streaming down, they watered the ground under her eyes in every place where she prayed." She had so abhorred and detested the blasphemies of her son that she felt she could not live in the same house with him. But God changed her mind and consoled her anguish through a dream which assured her of his ultimate salvation.

"For almost nine years passed, in which I wallowed in the mire of that deep pit, and the darkness of falsehood, often assaying to rise, but dashed down the more grievously. All which time that chaste, godly, and sober widow (such as Thou lovest), now more cheered with hope, yet no whit relaxing in her weeping and mourning, ceased not at all hours of her devotions to bewail my case unto Thee. And her *prayers entered into Thy presence,* and yet Thou sufferedst me to be yet involved and reinvolved in that darkness" (Book III, [XI] 19, 20).

In the spiritual realm there must always be a breaking-up and breaking-down before the inwrought life is free for use. Those who sow in tears are promised that they shall reap in joy. But for long years prayer may seem to effect nothing.

When Gideon was told to attack the Midianites the pitchers had to be shattered before the light could shine. Paul must have had that story in mind when he wrote of our being mere clay pots, but with a priceless treasure, the light of the knowledge of the glory of God within. He who knew many kinds of shattering has shed a strong light down through the ages.

A woman who has brought the light of the Lord to many sexually abused girls wrote to me of the anger and hurt they feel towards the heavenly Father who was supposed to protect them from every evil thing and did not. It did not surprise me to learn that this woman, too, has been broken—twice divorced, has a handicapped child, is tormented by unrelenting pain which interrupts her sleep and draws her mind from work (she is the wage-earner for her family). She recognized in herself a "pool of hurt," felt unloved and rejected by God, but kept these feelings, she said, "out in the light before Him," and He began to teach her His love.

> I totally agree with your statement about accepting suffering as a gift and about offering it up to the Lord. At times of intense emotional or physical pain I have actually envisioned a chalice full of suffering, lifted to the Lord as the only offering I could bring. When suffering is intense enough, it overtakes all of life until that is all one has (ask a woman in the last stages of a difficult delivery—or *any* delivery!). Embrace it, then offer it up.... As the pain would begin to crest (sometimes many times in a few minutes) I would internally stop and draw apart to worship, not *asking* the Lord for anything, just expressing my love for Him. I noticed the tension and stress of carrying constant pain would subside.

So the testimony comes from every age, from all over the world—suffering is necessary. Suffering is the key to existence. Suffering opens our eyes to the centrality of the cross in the Christian life, enables us to lift up the crucified Savior to the rest of the world. How thankful I am for those who have shown us so clearly that the pathway through suffering leads on to glorious things.

Lilias Trotter shows how, out of the hour of its greatest extremity, the seed launches out for its ministry. When all seems to be lifeless, all that is beautiful withdrawn and shrouded, the invisible, miracle-working power of God has not come to a halt. It operates silently, secretly in the seed, and in us. "It is the Spirit that gives life, the flesh is of no avail; the words that I have spoken to you are spirit and life. But there are some of you who do not believe" (Jn 6:63-64, RSV).

It happened that I was working on the outline for this chapter in a motel room in California, struck by the wonder of the hidden life of the seed. The One who designed it showed to the young English artist in the deserts of North Africa the deep lessons from the life cycle of desert flora which illuminated her sufferings. She in turn faithfully wrote of these lessons more than half a century ago and here I was, thirstily drinking them in from her little book for perhaps the tenth time, sitting with my feet propped on a chair and a clipboard on my lap. The phone rang. It was Walt, my son-in-law, asking for help with a letter he was trying to write. The notes on my clipboard from *Parables of the Christ-Life* were the very words he needed at that moment.

Thus the Life multiplies—but only because the seed fell into the ground and died. Lilias Trotter had no idea how far the golden grain would be scattered.

The light is shed abroad—because the vessel was broken.

God gave to the widow of Zarephath her poverty, that out of her poverty she might give something to His prophet. God gave to Joseph through his sufferings the power to save the lives of the brothers who had hated him. He named his son Ephraim because "God has made me fruitful in the land of my hardships" (Gn 41:52). God gave Paul his thorn, gave him the happiness of suffering for other Christians. Jesus spoke of His own cup of suffering as the cup which the Father had *given* Him.

Is it too hard for us to believe that the Shepherd who leads in paths of righteousness has good reason to lead us in the pathway of suffering? Too hard to believe His word, "This day, as ever, thy decrees stand fast; for all things serve thee" (Ps

119:91)? Too hard to believe that God is giving us gifts—from which, by His transfiguring power, will come something that will matter very much not only to us but to others as well?

Lord, I believe. Help my unbelief.

TWENTY-FOUR

The Divine Schedule
Is Flawless

here is a definite moment at which the seed is ripe for being liberated. . . . All prepared are the hooks or spikes or gummy secretions needed to anchor it to the ground, and so to give purchase to the embryo shoot when the time comes for it to heave its tombstone and come out into the light.

Even its center of gravity is so adjusted that, in falling from the sheath, the germ is in the very position for its future growth. If it is torn out of the husk a day too soon, all this marvelous preparation will be wasted and come to naught.

WHEN SATAN ACCOSTED JESUS IN THE WILDERNESS he set before Him three temptations, in each of which lay the possibility of good or evil (could the spotless Son of God have been tempted by pure and unmitigated evil? "I do not believe that the Son of God could be tempted with evil, but I do believe that he could be tempted with good—to yield to which temptation would have been evil in him and ruin to the universe" [George MacDonald: *Unspoken Sermons*, Longmans, Green, and Co., London, 1906, p. 134]]. The third was perhaps the most powerful of the three temptations. Jesus was offered possession of all the kingdoms of the world and their magnificence if He would worship Satan. What might He not have done with such power? Grand thoughts of replacing a corrupt government with a righteous one, filling the world with the knowledge of the Lord as the waters cover the sea, wiping away all tears, preaching good news to the poor, releasing captives, recovering sight to the blind, setting at liberty the oppressed—all this might have tempted him to take up the offer, but it was not the way appointed. He had arrived in our world in utter weakness. He would be limited by time and space as any of us are limited. He would walk its roads as anyone walks, be tired and thirsty, misquoted, misunderstood, scorned, rejected, and hated. He would be captured, bound, slapped, flogged, blindfolded, crowned with thorns, stripped, and nailed—in *weakness*, Scripture says (2 Cor 13:4)—to a cross.

All this He might have avoided by accepting Satan's offers. Why should anyone *choose* the pathway of suffering if another way is offered? Jesus had come for one reason and one only—to do the Father's will—and He set His face like a flint to do just that, in perfect harmony with that will, seeking not to sidestep or skip any part of it nor to find a quicker, easier route. He would, like the seed with its center of gravity perfectly adjusted, quietly awaiting the perfect moment for its work, abide faithfully by God's way and God's timing.

His followers understand this.

Paul Schneider, a German pastor born in 1897, refused to fall in with the course of Hitler's regime and after repeated threats and arrests, was taken to Buchenwald, leaving behind his wife and six children. On account of his refusal to salute the swastika he was placed in solitary confinement in the infamous "Bunker." A year of unbroken torture killed him in 1939. Before he was taken to Buchenwald he wrote to his wife that the die was cast and he had been sentenced to a concentration camp. A friendly jailer allowed him to write a last letter:

"As we have done until now, so in the future we want to trust God alone, in lowliness and patience to expect from Him alone everything good, and Him alone love, fear, and honor with our whole hearts. Thus God will be with us, and we will not be brought to shame in our hope. Be comforted and faithful and do not be fearful. I keep you all close in my heart. In God we are not separated. Be heartily thankful for all the love after this. We want to be thankful for this beautiful time of preparation for harder tests. New sufferings should bring us new experiences of our God and new splendors.

Christ speaks: "I am with you every day, always . . . ,"

In love, your Paul."

Those who, like Paul Schneider and his Master, fling soul and body down in joyful abandonment to whatever choice the Father may make for them, rest in the confidence that God will make no errors, in timing or anything else. Jesus was aware when He was at the wedding in Cana that his *hour* had not yet come. He knew when it did come. Just after His entrance into Jerusalem He said it was *time* for the Son of Man to be glorified—to become, not the king the crowds had hailed with hosannas but a grain of wheat that must die. In Gethsemane

He said to the weary disciples, "The hour has come. The Son of Man is betrayed to sinful men. Up, let us go forward; the traitor is upon us" (Mt 26:45-46). He made no effort to escape. When the mob, led by Judas, came after Him with swords and clubs He walked straight up to them and asked who it was they wanted.

"Jesus of Nazareth" was the answer, which so stunned them that they fell to the ground. Day after day, when He had been with them in the temple, none had laid a hand on Him. But the moment had arrived, "the hour when darkness reigns" (Lk 22:53).

And so it was, in the fullness of time, at a particular moment in human history, on a particular Friday when one Pontius Pilate was procurator of Judea, that His work on earth culminated on a particular hill outside the wall of Jerusalem. As there is a definite moment at which the seed is absolutely ready for its fall, its hooks prepared, its center of gravity adjusted, everything done in cooperation with the forces of nature, so the death He was to die, as though He were a common criminal, took place in political and religious circumstances over which His Father had sovereign control. Darkness was allowed to reign.

Christ's YES to Satan's offer in the wilderness would have meant a quick and easy pathway to one kind of glory. It would also have meant NO to the Father's will. YES to His will and NO to Satan meant a pathway straight to the Cross. The prophet Isaiah, centuries earlier, described that pathway:

> Without beauty, without majesty (we saw him),
> no looks to attract our eyes;
> a thing despised and rejected by men,

❧

a man of sorrows and familiar with suffering,
a man to make people screen their faces;
he was despised and we took no account of him.

And yet ours were the sufferings he bore,
ours the sorrows he carried.
But we, we thought of him as someone punished,
struck by God, and brought low.
Yet he was pierced through for our faults,
crushed for our sins.
On him lies a punishment that brings us peace,
and through his wounds we are healed.

We had all gone astray like sheep,
each taking his own way,
and Yahweh burdened him
with the sins of all of us.
Harshly dealt with, he bore it humbly,
he never opened his mouth,
like a lamb that is led to the slaughter-house,
like a sheep that is dumb before its shearers
never opening its mouth.

By force and by law he was taken;
would anyone plead his cause?
Yes, he was torn away from the land of the living;
for our faults struck down in death.
They gave him a grave with the wicked,
a tomb with the rich,
though he had done no wrong
and there had been no perjury in his mouth.
Yahweh has been pleased to crush him with suffering.

If he offers his life in atonement,
he shall see his heirs, he shall have a long life
and through him what Yahweh wishes will be done.

His soul's anguish over
he shall see the light and be content.
By his sufferings shall my servant justify many,
taking their faults on himself.

Hence I will grant whole hordes for his tribute,
he shall divide the spoil with the mighty,
for surrendering himself to death
and letting himself be taken for a sinner,
while he was bearing the faults of many
and praying all the time for sinners.   (Is 53:2-12, JB).

The pathway of self-obliteration led to a glory and a majesty
that Satan with all the power he had offered to Christ in that
wilderness scene could never have counterfeited.

"That is why God has now lifted Him to the heights, and has
given him the name beyond all names, so that at the name of
Jesus 'every knee shall bow,' whether in Heaven or earth or
under the earth. And that is why, in the end, 'every tongue shall
confess' that Jesus Christ is the Lord, to the glory of God the
Father" (Phil 2:9-11, JBP).

TWENTY-FIVE

A Home within the Wilderness

he seeds [of the cranesbill] stand together as they ripen, like arrows in a quiver, with their points downward, and their feathered shafts straight up. When the time for action comes, the sun-heat peels them off, from below and above, so quickly that you can see them curl under your eyes, and turn into a spiral by their continued contractions.

They fall, spike downward, by the weight of the seed, and the sun finishes the work he began. Closer still the gimlet winds, and as it does so it bores down into the hardest soil. Such is their strange power of penetration, as they are driven in spite of their weakness, that they bury themselves up to the very hilt, leaving only the last long curve flat on the surface. Then this snaps off, leaving the head deeply hidden.

IS THE CHRISTIAN LIFE ALL SACRIFICE and sorrow and suffering? No, a thousand times no. The very ones who have known most of sacrifice and sorrow and suffering testify most unequivocally of joy and peace and blessing, for they have discovered in it the "key to existence." Is it too late for us who take for granted the tremendous privileges and appalling luxuries of our country to grasp this treasure?

My Hungarian friend is convinced that I, together with most Westerners, exaggerate the hardness of the situation in her country. I suppose she is right—the contrasts are shocking to the casual visitor. She says:

"I have never in my life experienced any hardship on this account. All the hardships and sufferings I have been through were entirely private and personal and could have happened to me in any country. I have been to America and I have a basis for comparison. The only thing I could envy of you is the incomparably higher standard of living, that famous convenience which characterizes American society. No, I don't deny I live in a country where negligence, disorganization, bureaucracy, administration, laziness, the economic crisis, and all the rest do their best to embitter one's life. At least in this field I am not spoiled, so spiritually I don't lose, but even gain. I often smile at naive Western young people who know nothing at all about facing housing problems as a young married couple with nowhere to live, who travel from London to Amsterdam and back as I travel from Budapest to Lake Balaton, who are outraged when they have to eat too many eggs and red meat which will spoil their precious health. How will these people ever learn what it is to renounce something and be content with what they have? I am rather ashamed because I live in abundance while people in Transylvania starve. Life has never been unbearable here, and being a Hungarian compensates for all. I love my country."

Another Eastern European asked me if I thought America could learn anything from the Christians in his country. I replied that I hoped those Christians might teach us the meaning of suffering, for we are "God's heirs and Christ's fellow-heirs, *if* we share his sufferings now in order to share his splendour hereafter" (Rom 8:17, italics mine). The message is clear: if we evade suffering, we shall miss out on the splendor. Jeremiah wrote, "If you have raced with men on foot and they have wearied you, how will you compete with horses? And if in a safe land you fall down, how will you do in the jungle of the Jordan?" (Jer 12:5, RSV).

If we are ever called to great suffering, how shall we bear it if we have not learned to share willingly with Christ our small ones? How shall we manage to save others if in little common ways we are bent on saving ourselves? Jesus could not do it ("He saved others, . . . he cannot save himself"—Mk 15:31). Neither can we.

The chance for each one of us to "die" is always given. The day's happenings are presented to us by the God who conceived the intricate shape of the cranesbill's seed. With exquisite delicacy He prepares us in mysterious ways and teaches us how to receive our daily deaths, whether they be small ones such as the cutting remark, the social slight, the unwelcome task, or the coming to pass of our worst fear.

A missionary to whom I had sent the tape of Lilias Trotter's book wrote:

"Listening to *Parables of the Cross* has confirmed the rightness of a recent fleeting glimpse into the mystery of the unseen. The cross which you both speak about has eluded my deeper understanding despite years of Christian education. The past years have offered a brutal but long overdue stripping of my profession and worth, confidence in relationships, and reputation for emotional stability under pressure."

Something happened which she did not describe. Then:

"Last week an edge was reached and the intellectual assent to suffering couldn't hold. I chose to step down from an appointed cross, flinging it aside by an act which seemed deceptively like survival at the time—flight.

"And a curious thing happened. A new misery descended, but one bringing insight rather than despair. For suddenly, out from under the cross's shadow, I felt exposed, unprotected. The freedom to quit, to choose not to love, remained, but the (dare I say) *comfort* of the cross was lost. That secret inner knowledge of a pulsating presence under the heaviness was gone; an unspoken covenant was broken. Christ stood dishonored by my hand. The channel of His glory was removed.

"I thought immediately of Mark 8:34, the imperative of TAKE UP the personal cross. If it had at one time been laid upon me, now it was definitely mine to choose to take—for His sake and mine. And I prayed, 'Restore the cross to me,' a shocking request, considering the severity of pain, considering the history of complaining.

"And it was restored, only heavier. But this time jealously embraced, albeit with feebleness, and it was as if I'd come 'home.' This familiar niche of suffering became a desired haven, the required obedience a welcomed task. No one could have been more surprised. Now maybe He can speak words I'm finally ready to hear. This cosmic partnership has been re-yoked."

I have nearly worn this letter out rereading it. I have carried it around with me, studied it, shared it with others, prayed for its lesson to sink deeply into my own heart. What a phrase, "the *comfort* of the cross"! I have begun to understand much better the words of a favorite hymn, Elizabeth Clephane's "Beneath the Cross of Jesus":

a home within the wilderness,
a rest upon the way ...

and especially the words of the stanza commonly omitted from modern hymnals:

Oh, safe and happy shelter!
Oh, refuge tried and sweet!
Oh, trysting place where heaven's love
And heaven's justice meet.

Home. Rest. Shelter. Refuge. This cross, this instrument of execution, these crossbeams of real wood, these nails of real iron—here and here alone will we find the key to suffering, the key to our very existence on this sorely wounded planet. Jesus Christ, whose real human flesh submitted to the lashes, the thorns, and the nails, transfigured that cross by His whole-hearted surrender to it in *love*—love for His Father, love for us, His helpless, sinning, suffering, despairing children.

But, we say, there are different categories of suffering—some of them are because we are faithful followers of Christ, some the woes and misfortunes common to our human race, but many are the direct result of our own sin. We reap what we sow. Must we not simply grin and bear the sufferings in the last category? Can we expect God to waive punishment which we richly deserve?

We must remember first of all that He took it *all*—all the

punishment for all the sin of all the world. He paid the full price. He, the Lamb slain before the foundation of the world, suffered for us then and suffers with us now, regardless of the source of our trouble. If we suffer, He suffers.

We must also remember that actions have consequences to which, as long as we live on this earth, we cannot be immune. All punishment, all discipline from God is from a loving Father whose sole object is to make us like Himself—holy. So let us receive it humbly, trusting in His love—a far cry from mere grinning and bearing. Of course we do not always know, while in the middle of it, to which category our suffering belongs. Often it is a mixture, but the cross remains our refuge nonetheless.

I listened to a divorced man's story of his disillusionment with his wife, her failures, her heartlessness, her shattering of his image of what he thought he was getting.

"Why would God have me marry somebody like that? I prayed about it. I thought she was a Christian. I thought she would love me as I wanted to be loved. I couldn't stand it. I endured years of loneliness—*terrible* loneliness. I don't know if you know what that's like."

Was any of the fault his? How much of it? Had he loved her as Christ loved the church? Had he laid down his life for her? Did he deserve any of the treatment he got? What kind of treatment did she get from him? I did not know the answers, nor could I ask him the questions. It was too late to mend the marriage. She has long since remarried, while he continues to stare at the "poor hand of cards" he's been dealt. What then could I say? *You will find peace only in the cross. Take it all to the cross and leave it there.* I did my best to explain what I believe that means: forgive her, ask her forgiveness, ask God to teach you whatever you need to learn through the price you are having to pay.

The disorders and sorrows in my own life, whether attributable solely to my own fault, solely to somebody else's, perhaps to a mixture of both, or to neither, have given me the chance to learn a little more each time of the meaning of the cross. What can I do with the sins of others? Nothing but what I do with my own—and what Jesus did with all of them—take them to the cross. Put them down at the foot and let them stay there. The cross has become my home, my rest, my shelter, my refuge.

TWENTY-SIX

For the Joy Set Before

*T*hink about the golden plough of the wild oat, with every spike and hair so set that it slips forward and will not be pushed backward. "He steadfastly set His face toward Jerusalem"—and the Cross.

TALKING ON THE PHONE with my daughter Valerie one day I heard howling and singing in the background.

"What's happening?" I asked.

"Oh that's Elisabeth, singing in the bathroom to try to cheer up Jim who doesn't want his ears scrubbed!"

Elisabeth was seven, Jim two. I asked what she was singing.

Because He lives, I can face tomorrow,
Because He lives, all fear is gone.
Because I know He holds the future,
And life is worth the living just because
He lives!

A two-year-old has to howl sometimes. Singing about the resurrection to a little boy with soap in his eyes is adding insult to injury. We know how this feels.

The resurrection, however, is the anchor of our hope. We know that heaven is not *here*, it's *there*. If we were given all we wanted here, our hearts would settle for this world rather than the next. Through myriad variations of "soap in the eyes" God is forever luring us up and away from this kingdom of pain, wooing us to Himself and His still invisible Kingdom where what we so keenly long for we shall, if we stoop to enter the small gate, most certainly find.

"And God himself will be with them; he will wipe away every tear from their eyes, and death shall be no more, neither shall there be mourning nor crying nor pain any more, for the former things have passed away" (Rv 21:3-4, RSV).

The Bible begins with perfection and ends with perfection, but in between is the saga of man's sin and God's mercy, the mercy that endures forever, reaching down to loved sinners. The story is faithful to the dark side and the bright side, to blatant disobedience and heroic obedience, chaos and order, suffering and joy—it's all in there, with God the Father standing always within the shadows, keeping watch above His own.

Joseph was the victim of his brothers' jealousy and a rejected seductress's fury, but through many years of suffering God brought about the salvation of His people.

Esther, a beautiful Jewish virgin in the harem of a Persian king, risked her life to save her people when the king issued an order to exterminate them.

Daniel, in a den of lions for refusal to obey a heathen king's orders, stands as one of the towering heroes whose deeds speak louder than any sermon, making visible to us that faith in God means obedience with no thought of consequences. It means not only do *or* die but sometimes do *and* die. Daniel was ready for either.

For Jonah the horror chamber of a fish's stomach became the place of spiritual illumination and repentance.

Paul's prison chains made the Philippian Christians more confident in the Lord, more bold to speak the word of God without fear. An unnamed illness led to his bringing the gospel to the Galatians.

For all these there must have been excruciating emotional suffering. We can try to put ourselves in the pit or the prison with Joseph. We can imagine to some degree how Esther's heart was in her mouth as she waited to see if the king would receive her. Listen with Daniel to the heart-stopping snarling of the lions—at what moment will the first one spring out of the blackness? Smell and feel with Jonah the fetid slime of a marine animal's digestive tract. Lie in the filth of the prison with Paul. Although the physical suffering was great, the mental and emotional suffering must have exceeded it—how long will this go on? Will I be able to endure? What will the end be? Has God forgotten me?

Many modern afflictions fall into this category—abandonment by parents or spouse, depression and mental illness, the scourges of addiction or homosexuality in someone we love, the indelible memory of sexual abuse.

Is there no balm for such pain? The fragrance of the balm of Gilead permeates the sacred story. Men and women in fear and pain and helplessness of all kinds found solace and peace. That balm has not lost its restorative power. A woman whose childhood was filled with indescribable abuse and defilement shared with me three principles which had revolutionized her life. I who had no such past am glad she permits me to share them with you.

1. Forgiveness—Mark 11:25—is essential. It is so insidiously pleasant to hold onto the "right" to feel angry, hurt, depressed, vengeful, etc. Unless we forgive our childhood tormentors the way Jesus forgave us as we tormented Him on the cross, we will never have any spiritual freedom in our lives. This is merely an act of the will. We must *will* to forgive them and God works the forgiveness in our hearts.

2. Trust in God's sovereignty—Genesis 50:20. If I am going to trust God for my *future* then I must trust His sovereignty over my *past*. He could have prevented it. He allowed it to happen. He makes no mistakes. He hath done all things well.

To consider the life of Joseph makes it impossible to complain about the "injustices" in our lives. Human injustice is a mere chisel in the hand of God. The instrument may seem sharp and cruel but the Sculptor is the epitome of kindness and love.

3. Having a view to eternity—Colossians 3:1-4. This life is nothing but a vapor. My childhood must be less than a blink of the eye. I have all of now and forever to enjoy God's love and the wonderful things He has planned for me. Perhaps one of Satan's craftiest tricks in this age of psychoanalysis is to keep us focused inward. The Word tells us to focus upward, put off the old man, put on the new and *go*.

A few of the Scriptures which helped her were these:
"When my father and my mother forsake me, then the Lord

will take me up" (Ps 27:10, AV).

"Can a woman forget her nursing child, that she should not have compassion on the son of her womb? Yea, they may forget, yet will I not forget thee. Behold, I have engraved thee upon the palms of my hands" (Is 49:15, 16).

"Be not overcome of evil, but overcome evil with good" (Rom 12:21, AV).

"Brethren, I count not myself to have apprehended: but this one thing I do, forgetting those things which are behind, and reaching forth unto those things which are before, I press toward the mark for the prize of the high calling of God in Christ Jesus" (Phil 3:13-14).

This, I believe, is what it means to *embrace* the cross. Here is a woman who has found in her own childhood tragedy the presence and the transcendence of God. Her ears have been open to His word, and by a profound and peaceful acceptance of an unspeakable experience and a humble self-donation she has received in exchange His grace which enables her to forgive, to trust, to fix her eyes on the invisible.

The Lord of Heaven desires and seeks our companionship (remember His words to the disciples, "Will you also go away?"), but we can never go far along the road if we refuse things that are hard for us. Our spiritual apprenticeship is served only as we earnestly observe what the Master does and do it after Him, not asking for shelter from winds that beat on Him, but turning our faces to that wind, taking up and embracing His cross.

A glad acceptance of hard things opens the way for glory. In John's great vision of the rainbow-circled throne from which went out flashes of lightning and peals of thunder, he wept because there was no one worthy to open the scroll held by the One on the throne. One of the elders says to him, "Do not weep, for the Lion from the tribe of Judah, the Scion of David, has won the right to open the scroll and break its seven seals" (Rv 5:5). Then John saw, not the golden-maned king of the beasts with burning eyes and swinging tail, but a little lamb, all bloodied as though it had been sacrificed. When the Lamb took the scroll the living creatures and the elders around the throne fell down before Him and sang a new song—He was worthy to take the scroll because He had shed His blood. Then the Seer hears the voices of angels, thousands upon thousands, shouting, "Worthy is the Lamb, the Lamb that was slain, to receive all power and wealth, wisdom and might, honour and glory and praise!" (Rv 5:12).

All that the world so desperately seeks the Lamb won, not by aggression but by surrender. That is the principle of the cross. It takes the weak and makes them strong. It takes our sin and bestows Christ's righteousness. Out of bondage we are made free. Darkness is overcome by light. Loss turns into gain.

Perhaps this page is read by someone who feels pinned down by depression, immobile, hating himself, worthy of nothing but the trash pile. People offer their cheerful little remedies and succeed only in arousing hostility and strengthening the conviction that it's all over, there is no answer. Life is all husk.

Long before John wrote the Book of the Revelation, the prophets had written of wonderful exchanges—Isaiah wrote of pine trees and myrtles replacing camel thorns and briars; of God's giving garlands instead of ashes, oil of gladness instead of mourners' tears, a garment of splendor for a heavy heart (Is 61:3). Nehemiah wrote of blessings where there had been cursing; the psalmist of dancing and joy where there had been laments and of pasture instead of wilderness. Were these mere visions of unreality?

Jesus spoke of transformations. The poor, the sorrowful, the hungry and thirsty, the persecuted would be happy, would inherit the Kingdom of Heaven, find consolation, be satisfied, have rich rewards. Was He offering only a carrot on a stick?

The apostle Paul was carried away with the prospects—the perishable to become imperishable, weakness to be turned into power, humiliation to glory, mortality to immortality, poverty to riches, vile bodies to resplendent ones, the curse of the law replaced by the blessing of Abraham. Was it truth or poetry?

Think of the golden plough of the wild oat, every spike and hair so set that it slips forward and will not be pushed backward. Why? There is a golden harvest ahead. And Jesus, for the joy that was set before Him, accepted, embraced, and endured the cross. And for all who follow hard after Him, faces set as His was, "like a flint," refusing to be pushed backward, that same joy is in store, for He prayed "that they may have my joy within them in full measure" (Jn 17:13).

TWENTY-SEVEN

There Shall Be No More Night

*B*ut all is on the very verge of a flood-tide of life, for the seed-vessel has reached its highest ministry now. The last wrappings are torn and from every rent and breach the bare grain is shed forth and brought into direct contact with the soil. Suddenly, as if by miracle, the quickening comes, and the emerald shoot is to be seen.

THE MESSAGE OF THE TINY SEED interprets human life. Without it suffering remains an inscrutable mystery. The great Corn of Wheat showed forth the meaning of love by suffering.

If we have never sought, we seek Thee now;
Thine eyes burn through the dark, our only stars;
We must have sight of thorn-pricks on Thy brow,
We must have Thee, O Jesus of the Scars.

The heavens frighten us; they are too calm.
In all the universe we have no place.
Our wounds are hurting us—where is the balm?
Lord Jesus, by Thy scars, we claim Thy grace.

The other gods were strong, but Thou wast weak.
They rode, but Thou didst stumble to a throne.
But to our wounds only God's wounds can speak,
And not a god has wounds but Thou alone.

(Edward Shillito [source unknown])

As thousands have testified, were it not for wounds they would never have known so deeply Him whose wounds speak. Thomas refused to believe in the Christ of the Resurrection until He showed them His hands and His feet. "We must have Thee, O Jesus of the Scars."

We bow in gratitude for His willingness to take the cup the Father gave Him, a cup so immensely more bitter than the one He gives us. Shall we refuse it, or shall we grasp it with both hands, as it were, realizing it holds just what is most needful for our spiritual wholeness? Ours has been sweetened, as Rutherford put it, "at the lip of sweet Jesus." We drink it—by trustful acceptance—and God transforms it for His glory. Thus our very suffering may become the substance of sacrifice—a love-offering to God and a sacrifice of praise, and our ambition may be changed as radically as was Paul's, who said,

"All I care for is to know Christ, to experience the power of his resurrection, and to share his sufferings, in growing conformity with his death" (Phil 3:10).

We are on the very verge of a floodtide of life. The miracle will come, we do not know the moment, but "his servants shall worship him; they shall see him face to face, and bear his name on their foreheads. There shall be no more night, nor will they need the light of lamp or sun, for the Lord God will give them light; and they shall reign for evermore" (Rv 22:3-5).

A Summary of Reasons for Suffering

or the Lord will not cast off for ever, but, though he cause grief, he will have compassion according to the abundance of his steadfast love; for he does not willingly afflict or grieve the sons of men.

(Lam 3:31-33, RSV)

WE MAY GROUP SOME OF GOD'S reasons into four categories. The list of references is by no means exhaustive.

First, we suffer for our own sake:

that we may learn who God is	Ps 46:1, 10; Dn 4:24-37; the Book of Job,
that we may learn to trust	2 Cor 1:8-9,
that we may learn to obey	Ps 119:67, 71,
discipline is proof of the Father's love and of the validity of our sonship	Heb 12:5-11,
it is the condition of discipleship	Acts 14:22; Lk 14:26-27, 33,
it is required of soldiers	2 Tm 2:4,

we are being "pruned" that we may bear fruit	Jn 15:2,
that we may be shaped to the image of Christ	Rom 8:29,
to qualify us to be fellow-heirs with Christ	Rom 8:17,
to qualify us for the kingdom of God	2 Thes 1:4-5,
to qualify us to reign with Christ	2 Tm 2:12,
that our faith may be strengthened	Jas 1:3; 2 Thes 1:4-5; Acts 14:22,
that faith may be tested and refined	Is 43:2; Dn 11:35; Mal 3:2; 1 Cor 3:13; 1 Pt 1:7,
that we may reach spiritual maturity	Jas 1:4,
power comes to its full strength in weakness	2 Cor 12:9,
to produce in us endurance, character, hope	Rom 5:3-4,
to produce in us joy and generosity	2 Cor 8:2.

Second, we suffer for the sake of God's people:

that they may obtain salvation	2 Tm 2:10,
to give them courage	Phil 1:14,
that because of death working in us, life may work in them	2 Cor 4:12; Gal 4:13; 1 Jn 3:16,
that grace may extend to more	2 Cor 4:15,
that our generosity may bless others	2 Cor 8:2.

Third, we suffer for the world's sake:

that it may be shown what love and obedience mean	the Book of Job; Jn 14:31; Mt 27:40-43,
that the life of Jesus may be visible in ordinary human flesh	2 Cor 4:10.

Fourth, we suffer for Christ's sake:

that we may be identified with Him in His crucifixion	Gal 2:20,
suffering is the corollary of faith	Ps 44:22; Acts 9:16 and 14:22; 2 Tm 3:12; Jn 15:18-21; 1 Thes 1:6 and 3:4,
that we may share His suffering	1 Pt 4:12-13; Phil 1:29, 2:17 and 3:8, 10; Col 1:24; 2 Tm 1:8; Heb 13:13,
that we may share His glory	Rom 8:17-18; Heb 2:9-10; 2 Cor 4:17.

Lilias Trotter's *Parables of the Cross* and *Parables of the Christ-Life* are available on tape, read by Elisabeth Elliot. Price: $12 (includes postage). Ask for Trotter Tapes:

Lars Gren
10 Strawberry Cove
Magnolia, MA 01930

❧

The Elisabeth Elliot Newsletter (published six times per year) contains articles on contemporary topics such as home-schooling, abortion issues, marriage and sex, widowhood and divorce, and the role of Christians in various social and political arenas. Also included are regular features such as questions and comments by readers, recommended reading, and Elisabeth's travel and speaking itinerary. It is supported entirely by donations, but it is sent to any who request it, whether they contribute or not. If you would like to help, a $7.00 donation will cover the cost of mailing the newsletter to you for one year. Those who send more than $7.00 are helping to support others who cannot afford to contribute. Send your name and mailing address to: *The Elisabeth Elliot Newsletter*, P.O. Box 7711, Ann Arbor, MI 48107.